Acclaim for **DR. HEIDI SQUIER KRAFT'S**
RULE NUMBER TWO

"Heidi Kraft has given us a rare, insightful look into today's bat-tlefield. It is personal, emotional, and unique. She captures a perspective that only a psychologist, mother, and officer on the front lines can describe. Every American needs to read this."

— General Anthony C. Zinni, USMC (Retired),
former commander of U.S. Central Command

Rule Number Two is one of the most amazing books I have ever read. It made me weep. It made me laugh. It made me proud. It is funny, sad, sweet, and powerful. It is this war's *M*A*S*H*."

— Lieutenant Colonel Dave Grossman, USA (Retired),
author of *On Killing* and *On Combat*

"Dr. Heidi Kraft shows what it takes to do clinical mental health work in a war zone: the wisdom of Solomon, the prac-ticality of Edison, the wit of Danny Kaye, and the iron of Chesty Puller."   — Jonathan Shay, MD, PhD, author of
Achilles in Vietnam and *Odysseus in America*

"The welcome mat for memoirs by veterans of operations Iraqi Freedom and Enduring Freedom might never wear out so long as they write with the sincerity of Heidi Squier Kraft.... She wins respect with genuine empathy."

— J. Ford Huffman, *Military Times*

"What comes through...is a notion that has become unfashionable: the idea of service. Rescuing the concept from the rah-rah language that too often surrounds it, Kraft presents the book just as she promises, less a record of her deeds than an attempt to honor those she served with. Her writing style is direct and honest, and every page provides evidence of the long-lasting effect her time in Iraq has had on her."

— Charles Taylor, *Bloomberg Review*

"*Rule Number Two* reads journal-like, but is clearly a work of careful consideration that balances skillfully the demands of immediacy her stories compel and the reflection necessary to make sense of these stories. Kraft will, you feel, come out of it because of the book, and you hope that her other patients will because of her help." — Michael Pugliese, *Motif Magazine*

"Kraft holds hands with men in surgery...counsels suicidal Marines and colonels torn between concern for their men and the need to appear in control. She worries about her children back home. And she worries about her own increasing emotional numbness in the face of trauma. Finally, Kraft returns home. A junior psychiatric technician finds her sitting at her desk. 'It's okay,' he tells her, in one of this affecting book's most affecting moments, 'if you're not okay.'"

— Susan Salter Reynolds,
Los Angeles Times

"A more accurate description of the realities of war than more traditional memoirs because it deals with the damage combat does to the psyches of men and women who fight—and how efforts to heal that damage can change the lives of combat veterans who treat them."

—Chris Amos, *Navy Times*

"A necessary but uncomfortable book for anyone wishing to understand." —Jay Freeman, *Booklist*

"*Rule Number Two* offers...simple stories of individual struggles seen through the eyes of a practitioner who endures the same assaults on sanity as those she treats, underscoring the truth that even those escaping physical harm in combat do not return whole. Neither patient nor provider is spared, a truth reflected in the book's title."

—Ann E. Yow, *Seattle Times*

"Emotional and powerful, *Rule Number Two* is a piece of work that is worth sitting down with. Not only does Kraft write about her own fear and how she had to employ every psychological trick she knew to cope, but she also writes about the men and women she came across in her seven months in the desert. This book is not just her story—it's all their stories."

—Mary Scott, *Palos Verdes Peninsula News*

"*Rule Number Two* is a culmination of simple stories which affect many soldiers' lives and their families. Dr. Kraft mentions some instances of horrifying helplessness, yet remarkable moments of hope in a desert war. The touch of a hand, the blood on boots, and just the right words . . . In war, as Dr. Kraft illustrates several times, the human condition is ever so fragile and deserves care."   —Mona Lisa Safai, *Suite 101*

RULE NUMBER TWO

Lessons I Learned
in a Combat Hospital

———————

DR. HEIDI SQUIER KRAFT

Foreword by W. C. Gregson

BACK BAY BOOKS
Little, Brown and Company
New York   Boston   London

Back Bay Books / Little, Brown and Company
Hachette Book Group
237 Park Avenue, New York, NY 10017
www.hachettebookgroup.com

Originally published in hardcover by Little, Brown and Company, October 2007
First Back Bay paperback edition, May 2012
Back Bay Books is an imprint of Little, Brown and Company. The Back Bay
Books name and logo are trademarks of Hachette Book Group, Inc.

The publisher is not responsible for websites (or their content) that are not
owned by the publisher.

The Hachette Speakers Bureau provides a wide range of authors for speaking
events. To find out more, go to www.hachettespeakersbureau.com or
call (866) 376-6591.

Library of Congress Cataloging-in-Publication Data
Kraft, Heidi Squier.
Rule number two : lessons I learned in a combat hospital /
by Heidi Squier Kraft. — 1st ed.
p. cm.
ISBN 978-0-316-06790-4 (hc) / 978-0-316-06791-1 (pb)
1. Kraft, Heidi Squier. 2. Iraq War, 2003– — Personal narratives, American.
3. Military psychiatry. 4. Psychologists — United States — Biography.
5. United States. Navy — Women — Biography. I. Title.
DS79.76.K73 2007
956.7044'37 — dc22   2007013078

10 9 8 7 6 5 4 3 2 1

Design by Bernard Klein

RRD-C

Printed in the United States of America

For Deb Dunham,
the mother of a hero

And for Mike "Cheez" Kraft,
my hero, then and now

This book is dedicated to the people of Alpha Surgical Company,
especially Karen Lovecchio, Bill Reynolds, Cat Kesler, Steve Noakes,
Katie Foster Saybolt, Jesse Patacsil, and Dextro Gob . . . from whom I
learned the meaning of the word *comrade;*

to the United States Marines
whose care was entrusted to us in Iraq;

and to Jason Bennett,
the finest doctor I have ever known, my partner in the desert,
and my friend forever.

Author's Note

The people, places, and events described in this book are based on my recollection of them, to the best of my memory's ability.

With the exception of Corporal Jason Dunham, the name — and all identifying characteristics — of every patient described in this book has been changed.

Foreword

An incredibly intense and special bond exists between Marines and the Navy medical personnel who serve with us. The medical officers and corpsmen, our beloved docs, are not graduates of Marine boot camp or combat training. They are medical professionals with brief orientations — a whole eight days — to the operational environment. The Marines protect them like the royalty they are. They handle everything from preventive medicine, routine sick call, and dental care to emergency response and surgery. They bind our physical wounds and just as surely salve our mental casualties. They share our risks and revel in our successes. They weep with us, often for us, over our losses.

This is the story of one deployment of one medical officer — a mother and the wife of a Marine — who also happened to be a Navy psychologist. She was deployed to Iraq to care for the Marines and the medical personnel.

It is a very personal story, but it is also the story of all the men and women of the Navy and the Marine Corps in Al Anbar province in Iraq. Behind the newscasts and the headlines lie the real lives of the warrior class of America, many now on their third or fourth tour in Iraq. *Rule Number Two* is the story of the strong men and women who are doing the nation's bidding so that others may pursue their lives undisturbed.

W. C. Gregson
Lieutenant General (Retired)
United States Marine Corps

RULE NUMBER TWO

Prologue

September 2006

My dear Brian and Megan,

You were fifteen months old. You don't remember.

On an isolated air base in Iraq, somewhere between the Sunni triangle and the Syrian border, a small group of U.S. Navy doctors, nurses, and hospital corpsmen attempted to stabilize the trauma of war. They ducked their heads and ran to the helicopters that landed in their hospital's backyard. They unloaded wounded U.S. Marines, put them on stretchers, and carried them to waiting triage teams. They battled, day after day, the same grief and fear they saw in the eyes of their patients.

A tiny team among these Sailors — made up of a psychiatrist, a clinical psychologist, and two psychiatric technicians — provided mental health care for over ten thousand Marines in western Iraq. For nearly eight months, these four people fought to keep their patients, and one another, functional. They found themselves leading trauma interventions that were different from anything they had ever studied. It quickly became evident that combat mental health was anything but an exact science, and they strove to provide individual moments of comfort amid the chaos. They worked alongside their patients to uncover those wounds that surgeons would never see.

I was the psychologist on that team.

Your daddy, who flew attack jets in the Marine Corps for eleven years, gave me a card the day I left for Iraq. In that card, he wrote that he was proud of me for taking care of the men and women of the greatest fighting force in history. I packed my bags, and we all said good-bye.

I left your daddy there — with the generous help of your grandparents, who left their home and their lives to come and live with you — to take care of you, my children, so I could go halfway around the world to take care of someone else's.

I returned home just before your second birthday. It was the most difficult thing I have ever experienced, trying to reconnect with a Marine husband who had faced the unique challenge of staying back while his wife went to war and with children who had truly grown up while I was gone. One day, I started writing about those eight months away from you. Originally, I thought I would want to forget my time in Iraq. It turns out I was wrong.

I wanted to remember the pride of serving with the most extraordinary people I have ever known, so I would always treasure those friendships. I wanted to remember the grief of watching young men die and the anguish of telling their friends of their loss so I would never again take the gift of life for granted. Most of all, I wanted to remember the courage and the character of the Marines whose care was entrusted to me, so their sacrifice would be known to as many as I could tell.

Above all, I wanted to share those things with you.

Some of the memories I've included here for you are very sad, as they tell tales of great loss. War is traumatic, and that trauma is illustrated in some of these pages. While I was in Iraq, I learned firsthand about the cost of combat. And about the price of freedom.

I wrote this book so that the sacrifices of the Marines who fought in Iraq, and of the Sailors who took care of those Marines, would be remembered.

And I wrote it with the hope that you will both be able to understand, at last, why I had to go.

I will always love you.

Mommy

The Beginning,
Part I

Pagers have come a long way. When I was an intern ten years ago, our beepers produced a horrible, shrill sound — unsuitable for the human ear and audible to anyone who happened to be within a half-mile radius. By January of 2004, when I served as a staff clinical psychologist at Naval Hospital Jacksonville, my pager seemed downright polite, its muted singsong alert barely perceptible across the room.

Even that benign tune, however, sounded harsh and annoying in the middle of the night — exponentially so if I was on vacation.

My mom and dad had traveled from California to spend postholiday quality time in Florida with their fourteen-month-old twin grandchildren. I took five days off — in truth, largely to spend an entire week watching my parents watch my children.

One night during their visit, the peal of my pager awakened me at 0300. I staggered to the kitchen, splashed water on my face, turned on all the lights, and dialed the number displayed on the beeper. The resident in the emergency room told me about one of my patients, a very young Sailor who was about to become a very young single mother. At twenty-two weeks pregnant, she had experienced dangerous preterm labor, and as a precaution she had been admitted to a civilian hospital that would be able to care for a premature baby.

As the resident's voice rambled on, I sank into a chair at the kitchen table and lowered my forehead to my palm. I was always striving to separate the feelings of a clinician, who made decisions rationally and calmly, from those of a woman and mother, who sometimes did not. This became more challenging at 0300. Inhaling deeply, I closed my eyes and counted to five, slowing my heart rate before exhaling. With a sense of renewed control, I decided to visit my patient in the hospital the next morning, and I returned to bed.

Four hours later, I woke out of fitful, anxious dreams about my babies with the sense that I could not ease their pain. Pain about what, I could not remember.

The obstetricians controlled my patient's labor, and her baby remained safely in her womb. Relieved, I left the hospital midmorning, arriving on base in time for a farewell luncheon for our department head, Captain Goldberg. The four psychologists in the department, who had become one another's trusted friends both in and out of the hospital, looked to the captain as a protector and role model. We would miss him terribly.

At lunch, Captain Goldberg talked about how the new conflict in Iraq might affect us. He had been with the Marines when they had pressed to Baghdad less than a year earlier. Home for seven months now, he still seemed far away sometimes.

"I pray that this war will not place any of you in harm's way and away from your families," he said, making eye contact with each of us. "There is no indication this will occur in the near future — but if the unexpected happens, I have faith in all of you, as psychologists and officers."

As we filed out after lunch, each of us stopped to say a personal good-bye.

"If I am called, sir," I told him quietly, "I will do my best to make you proud of me."

I drove home along the river. Feeling connected with God as I gazed at the sun sparkling on the water, I said a prayer for the men and women of this war. I thought of my father and his service in the Navy during both the Korea and Vietnam conflicts, about which he never spoke. I wondered if our Operation Iraqi Freedom veterans would come home to a different world.

I almost didn't hear the singsong tune of my pager over U2's "Sunday Bloody Sunday," which I always turn up too loud.

"You've got to be kidding me," I mumbled to myself, rolling my eyes at the sight of our department phone number on the display. I picked up my cell phone and dialed.

"Heidi?" Our new department head, a lieutenant commander psychiatrist, answered the phone directly. "I was the one who paged you."

"Hi, Elissa. What's up?"

"Are you driving?"

"Yes."

"You should probably pull over."

"Elissa, what's going on? Is everyone okay?"

"Everyone's fine. But you should pull over."

"Okay, okay." I found a place to park along the riverfront road, under an ancient Florida shade tree whose leaves had been taken by winter. The afternoon sun already felt like spring.

I turned off the ignition and waited, my heart thumping audibly. She cleared her throat.

"Okay, I'm just going to say it. I got a call from the front office today. You have eleven days to report to Pendleton. Apparently, the West Coast psychologist who was supposed to deploy with First FSSG* has been pulled to do a float on a helicopter carrier. You're going in his place."

I sat in silence.

"Heidi?"

"I'm here."

I pulled into my garage with no recollection of the drive home. I sat motionless, staring at the dashboard for a few long minutes, and then I forced my muscles to move, gathered my things, and opened the door.

---

*Marine Corps First Service Support Group, now known as First Marine Logistics Group.

My mother and Meg, holding hands, emerged in the hall. My baby girl smiled when she saw me, her huge green eyes bright. I could hear my dad's animated voice as he read to Brian in another room. I crouched down, and Megan let go of her grandma to teeter across the ceramic tile into my outstretched arms. She circled my neck with tiny, warm hands.

"Ma-ma-ma-ma."

I held Megan tightly, tears flooding my eyes and spilling down my face. Looking over her shoulder, I met my mom's concerned eyes.

"Oh, no," she breathed. "Did something bad happen to your patient's baby?"

"No," I whispered, kissing the top of Meg's bald head. I shook my head and inhaled deeply.

"They're sending me to Iraq."

Alpha Surgical

I was not the only medical person who had been plucked from a stateside hospital to join the people of Alpha Surgical Company at Marine Corps Base Camp Pendleton as they prepared to deploy. In fact, only a handful of the personnel were actually organic to the overall medical battalion in peacetime; the majority of us were pulled from major Navy medical facilities to augment the mobile field hospitals.

I was, however, one of only two people who arrived at Camp Pendleton that first day, to find that Alpha Surgical Company had already left for Iraq.

Captain Sladek, a hematologist/oncologist in his twilight tour before retirement, and I had both been given erroneous reporting dates by our parent commands.

Upon the discovery that our unit was gone, the two of us were informed that we would prepare for deployment and travel into the theater with the personnel of our sister company, Bravo Surgical, which would be based at Fallujah. Once we arrived in Kuwait, we would be transported to Iraq to meet up with the company to which we actually belonged.

The captain and I began the transition process together,

enduring countless questions from everyone we encountered regarding why our names were not on the lists they had in front of them at the moment. We sat in the back, stood off to the side, and giggled at the fact that since no one knew we were there, no one would know if we disappeared. And yet there we stayed.

And there we sat, together on metal bleachers with Bravo Surgical, on the first of eight deployment training days at Marine Corps Base Camp Pendleton.

We were eighty Navy medical people — surgeons, physicians, psychologists, anesthesia providers, dentists, podiatrists, nurses, and hospital corpsmen, most of whom were based out of either Naval Medical Center San Diego or Naval Hospital Camp Pendleton. For the majority of us, this was our first experience preparing for combat operations of any kind, and we felt awkward and hesitant in the company of thousands of intense Marines.

In the week that followed, together we hauled empty seabags to fifteen different warehouses on base, methodically filling them to their brims with heavy combat gear. Together we donned gas masks and practiced in the gas chamber. Together we learned how to dismount a vehicle if a convoy was attacked and how to assist the Marines in the protection of that convoy. Most of us managed to deny we would need that one.

Together we were issued 9mm pistols and thirty rounds of ammunition.

At the end of the eight days, everyone wept or whispered

good-byes to their family members who had come before the sun rose to see them get on the bus. Everyone, that is, except Captain Sladek and me, whose families were across the country. I carried a farewell card from Mike, my Marine officer husband, in my cargo pocket. He wrote that he and my twins would be fine. He told me there were people who needed me more than they did right now.

So I stepped onto that bus with eighty people who swiped at tears and waved through the windows to their children. I put on my sunglasses, although it was still dark, and leaned my head back on the seat.

Several long and cold February flights later, we arrived at a base in Kuwait, a huge staging area for troops entering and exiting Iraq. For a little less than a week, close to a hundred females crammed into one tent, tucked our seabags under the cots that were lined up wall to wall, and attempted to find a way to pass the time.

It was during this week that I met Sandy, a pediatric surgeon with Bravo who had a two-year-old daughter. We became inseparable, talking about our children, our husbands, and our apprehension about what might lie ahead of us in Iraq. Several female Marine officers with cots nearby felt sorry for Sandy and me, I think, and they helped us learn to quickly clean and check our weapons. We washed our socks and underwear in the sinks in portable shower trailers since word to ship out could arrive at any moment and there was no time to use the laundry service. It was dark and very cold, and the wind howled at the canvas of the tent as we slept.

No one slept very well.

And then one day, when Sandy and I returned from breakfast, a Navy Chief met us at the entrance to our tent.

"Lieutenant Commander Kraft?"

"Yes." I hadn't met her before.

"I'm Chief Edmonson with Alpha Surgical. We've been waiting to get the remaining members of the company together before we make our push into country. We've got everyone now." She grinned at me.

"You ready, ma'am?"

It was a loaded question, of course. I had been sitting here in the sand of Kuwait doing nothing for six days. And yet now, faced with the moment I would actually load both seabags on the Humvee that would take us to the transport plane, I suddenly felt completely and totally unready.

I nodded.

Almost twenty-four hours later, our tiny group of stragglers arrived at Al Asad Airfield in Iraq in the chilling dead of night, and we hitched a ride on a Humvee to get to the hospital. Someone directed me to a dark room in which I was to drop my bags and find an open cot. I fell asleep with my boots on.

The light of day introduced me to the people of Alpha Surgical. When all was said and done, they had been in Iraq only about two weeks longer than Captain Sladek and me. I looked around, observing this newly founded band of medical and nurse officers and hospital corpsmen; I also observed the small group of men and one woman we came to call "our Marines." (Our Marines drove ambulances, operated radios, orchestrated communication, and arranged logistics for the unit — and they protected us.) I realized that, although it would have been nice to have been with all of them during those extra two weeks, it actually wasn't necessary. They were just like the people I'd met from Bravo: they had been mixed together, shipped across the world, and were now expected to function well as a mobile field surgical company in combat.

Somehow, despite the odds, we did. The infinite light brown dirt and rock of western Iraq quickly covered our boots. The first helicopter landed in the dust behind the hospital, and

HEIDI KRAFT

the first patients were hauled to our operating room. In those moments, we were transformed into a strangely familiar family, with serious personality conflicts, outright yelling matches, and seven-month grudges.

Yet we understood one another when it mattered. That's all our Marines knew. They knew they could count on us to take care of them. And somehow, even before we really knew them, we knew they would take care of us too.

Fever

Before the dawn of my third morning in country, I emerged sweat-soaked from vivid, disturbing dreams. I felt disoriented and nauseated, and a searing pain ripped across my shoulders and left arm. My head throbbed and my teeth ached. Frightened by the pain, I sat up, trying not to notice the walls shifting around me. I closed my eyes in an attempt to ease the dizziness and process the many sensations. The pain radiated from my left deltoid muscle, and suddenly I knew: it was the site of my smallpox vaccine, administered in Kuwait five days before our flight to Iraq.

I scanned the dark, windowless room. Five cots, five women, and ten seabags were crammed into a tiny exam area. Our assigned living quarters were still occupied, so we all lived in the hospital for our first weeks at Al Asad.

None of my sleeping roommates stirred as I swung my legs over the side of the cot. I squeezed my flashlight with one hand and, by its blue light, rummaged through my bag with the other. I found my shower gear and tiptoed out the door — so dizzy I almost fell, twice.

The shower in the hospital was located in a long, thin space with no lights, next to a broom closet. Just inside the door, a duct-taped X covered the bowl of a sink that had a long crack through its pedestal base. Beyond it, a small dressing area with three rotting wooden shelves on the walls led to a small square of tile flooring. A ceramic-coated hole in the tile functioned as a toilet, its flush handle protruding from the wall. A large plastic trash bag was crumpled in the corner, a repository for used toilet tissue, which the pipes could not handle. Most of the commodes at Al Asad were holes in the ground with bags next to them, but this one was special. It had a removable rusted metal grate cover, on which we were supposed to stand while the showerhead trickled water on us — and into the toilet.

I laid my flashlight on a wooden shelf to light up the shower area and immediately wished I had stayed in the dark. As soon as the water flowed, gigantic mosquitoes emerged from the grate and hovered around my head. Some things are better not seen.

Like my smallpox injection site. I gingerly removed the gauze that covered the wound and moved my arm into the light.

"Ohhhh," I groaned, looking away. The vaccine site, which I strove to keep clean and covered while it scabbed over, appeared bright red and angry. White fluid drained from its multiple punctures. Crimson tentacles stretched in all directions from the wound, going up my shoulder and across my chest, and also down that arm. I touched the surrounding skin with my right hand. It was hot.

The cold water felt wonderful on my flushed face. I washed the wound as well as I could, cringing through the pain. Slowly, clumsily, I dressed, fever and chills hitting me in alternating waves as I laced my boots.

I walked into the passageway and found a chair in the waiting area outside the exam rooms used for sick call, the non-emergent medical care we provided to the base. Today, I would be the patient. I sat and waited.

The sun rose and the people of Alpha Surgical Company rose with it, preparing the hospital for the day. Sometime after 0700, my friend Bill, one of two physician assistants in our company, left the call room and walked down the hall to set up his morning clinic. I raised a hand in hello.

He took one look at me and stopped walking.

"Wow, you look horrible."

"Thanks." I managed a smile. "I feel horrible." I peeled back the sleeve of my T-shirt and lifted the bandage.

Bill exhaled in a low whistle. "It's impossible to keep wounds clean out here. That looks bad." He ushered me into an exam room. My temperature had reached 103°.

Bill wrote me a prescription for antibiotics and ibuprofen. I smiled my thanks and moved to the small room we called a pharmacy, where one of the techs quickly filled a small Ziploc bag with pills.

"You're going to need to take the day off, by the way," Bill called over his shoulder at me as he entered an exam room.

"Thanks, I think I will." I downed two pills with bottled water and re-entered my temporary room, which was now empty. I collapsed on my cot, boots still laced and pistol still secure in the holster that hung from my shoulders.

My eyes flew open to the sound of pounding on my door.

"Lieutenant Commander Kraft? Are you in there?"

"Yes." My voice sounded unfamiliar. I cleared my throat and sat up. "Come in."

A corpsman from the ward opened the door and poked his head in the room.

"The CO [Commanding Officer] sent me to find you, ma'am."

I had no idea what time it was. I quickly ran a hand over my hair, which had dried postshower into clumps of matted curls as I slept. Thankfully already dressed, I stood — fighting dizziness — and followed him out. He starting jogging and looked back at me. Every cell in my body screamed in protest, but I caught up. He talked, out of breath, as we ran.

"Four Marines just got here — their vehicle hit a land mine out on a convoy. One has a pretty bad injury to his face. Dr. S. is not sure if he's going to be able to save his jaw, but he's going to the OR any minute to try. All four are still in the SST [Shock Stabilization Team]."

"Okay . . ." I waited.

"The reason we need you is that this colonel just showed up, their battalion CO, I guess. He's standing outside the SST. He's crying, ma'am. And he won't leave. Our CO told us to call you."

I stared at him.

"And this requires psych because . . . ?" I mumbled sarcastically to myself. If one of us was going to be called every time someone cried in the hospital, this had the potential to be a very long deployment.

He shrugged.

We arrived in the passageway outside the SST. The door to our makeshift emergency room was open, and scores of people wearing gloves and surgical masks moved around inside. Above the general hum of the voices of our SST personnel, another sound emerged.

A Marine was screaming.

His voice echoed through the passageways of the back of the hospital, a tortured cry made more heartbreaking by virtue of the fact that this nineteen-year-old man probably had never allowed himself to cry, let alone scream. Worse, his cries were contagious. His comrades had seen the gruesome injury to his face, and they heard his agony. They responded by calling to him, trying to drown out his shouts with their own words, support directed at him and exasperation directed at us.

"We're right here, Miller."

"You're doing great, buddy."

"Can't you *give* him something?"

Three Marine Corps officers hovered in the doorway of the SST, close enough to hear their men in pain but helpless to do anything about it. Two, identified by gold oak leaves on their collars as majors, appeared uncomfortable and slightly nauseated. The colonel stood between them. He was impossible to miss.

At least six-four, he towered over everyone around him. His dark hair was peppered with silver. He turned in my direction, and I could see that his blue eyes were bloodshot and his cheeks tear-streaked.

A litter team exited the SST and carried the Marine past the colonel, and he clearly saw the extent of the man's injuries. He watched as the stretcher turned the corner to the operating room.

The colonel turned to face the wall and placed a palm against the concrete, arm straight. He slowly lowered his head, and his big shoulders trembled as he began to sob.

I moved toward the three men, struck by the fact that both majors kept their distance from their leader but still watched him intently and with genuine concern. And suddenly I understood. Their concern was not for him.

As a commanding officer, the colonel was responsible for the welfare of these Marines. Several had been injured, one critically, and he could not change that. He was not in control, and control was usually the one thing he always had. He would have preferred to be injured himself rather than hear one of his men scream in pain. His anguish was palpable.

But he was not supposed to show it in public.

He wiped his eyes with his sleeve and turned to walk into the SST. I moved in front of him, blocking his entrance.

"Sir," I said, extending my hand. Surprised, he stopped and looked at me. "I am Heidi Kraft."

He shook my hand. The two majors approached out of curiosity.

"Why don't we just move over here, gentlemen." I turned them as a group and herded them toward the open door of the waiting area, away from the SST. One of my psych techs, Petty Officer Gob, stood nearby. I mouthed the word *Kleenex* to him, and he disappeared. The colonel hesitated, looking back toward the SST, where the moans of his Marines could still be heard.

"Please, sir." I locked eyes with him. The majors were already in the waiting room. "Please, come with me." Reluctantly, he followed me.

As we entered the waiting room, my face was on fire. I felt weaker every moment, my knees threatening to buckle beneath me. I handed the colonel a roll of toilet paper and sat across from him, leaning forward so that I could speak quietly. The majors sat across the room.

"Sir, I am one of the combat stress people here. Our surgical team asked me to help get you information. I will find out how your one Marine is doing in surgery and get you a status report on the other three." He nodded, tearing off some toilet tissue to blow his nose.

"When can I see them?" he asked.

"Once they are stabilized. Not before."

He lowered his eyes. "I understand."

I moved my face closer to his, my voice nearly a whisper.

"Sir, I want you to know that my team is here if *any* of your people should need us."

He looked directly at me. I was certain he could hear the hammering of my heart and that he knew I had trouble focusing on his face. *Please, God, don't let me pass out here in front of this colonel,* I thought. A brief look of understanding crossed his face. He nodded.

"Thank you, Heidi."

On any other day, he probably would have called me Lieutenant Commander Kraft or, much more likely, Doc. I smiled.

Two days later, my smallpox site looked better and my fever had broken. I felt like myself again and had the energy to walk to breakfast with Jason, our psychiatrist and my partner in our surgical company's Combat Stress Platoon. As we walked, I told him about my encounter with the colonel.

"To be honest, I'm not one hundred percent sure it happened that way," I admitted. "I was really feeling strange. Karen told me we ended up sending the guy with the jaw injury to Baghdad, since that level of repair was beyond our capability here. And she said the other three ended up being okay. So it appears those Marines were, in fact, actually here. But the whole thing still feels like a dream."

Jason nodded. Ever the psychoanalyst, he asked what, if the whole thing *had* been a dream, it might have been trying to tell me.

"I don't know . . . something about the definition of leadership, I suppose. Maybe that you couldn't pay me enough to be a Marine officer?"

I grinned at him. We entered the chow hall. "I'll tell you one thing, though. I understand now how terrifying it is to be sick or in pain out here. It's this completely scary, helpless, confused sensation. I never want to feel it again."

"The same sensation that every injured Marine who comes in here is feeling," Jason mused.

"Exactly."

"Good morning, Heidi."

The voice startled me, at once familiar and dreamlike. I turned to see the colonel, holding an empty tray as he entered the line behind us. I smiled at him.

"Good morning, sir."

That colonel said good morning to me in the chow hall nearly every morning for the next seven months.

And he always used my first name.

HOME

Brian and Megan started day care.

My father, a retired Navy submarine officer, composed an e-mail to me every day during my deployment and his extended stay with my husband and children. After about two weeks, the Internet cafés on our base actually functioned and we had figured out our schedules enough to find the time to stand in line for those precious thirty minutes on the computer. By the time I logged in for the first time, I had twenty messages waiting from him.

This labor of love included detailed accounts of the daily activities of our twins. Before I left, I begged him to do just that. Now, I found the words sent a shooting ice-pick sensation through me as I read. No one could have prepared me for the intensity of the pain. He wrote:

We are all getting up early each morning after Mike leaves for work, and have established a good morning routine.

The twins are starting to get the hang of the spoon — Meg cares about it more than Brian, who would still rather use his fingers. We take them in to school around 0830 each morning and pick them up before naptime, around 1100. They are adjusting very well to half days. Don't worry about us here — we're all doing fine.

Keep your head down.

Love, Dad.

Damn the Rockets

By just a little more than two weeks after our arrival in Iraq, we had unpacked our medical equipment, set up the hospital, and fixed the duty schedule. Helicopters landed on the dirt pad behind our building, delivering Marines wounded in firefights and by explosions from improvised explosive devices (IEDs). Final traces of the desert winter still lingered, and we used our cozy sleeping bags at night and wore fleece shirts under our utilities in the morning. (By noon they were history.) We should have enjoyed the sensation of cold while we had it. It would vanish within weeks of our arrival and would not return for seven months.

One evening in the middle of March, I sat on a cot with Jason. Together we leaned against the concrete wall and composed a plan on his laptop to assist with mental health coverage at another base. Bill and Steve, Jason's roommates, lay on their perpendicular cots watching *Mystic River* on Bill's computer. It was 2100. Outside, the moonless night was endless and black.

The first explosion was remote. It sounded similar to the distant booms produced by the Explosive Ordnance Disposal team (EOD) or by the firing of artillery. I looked up, and Jason stopped typing. His fingers had no sooner returned to the keyboard when another blast shook the air, closer this time. I became aware of a strange twisting sensation in my abdomen. Steve and Bill lifted both their heads in unison.

"What the fuck was that?" Steve asked, eyes darting to Jason and me. We all scrambled to our feet and rushed to the front hatch of the men's barracks. A small group of officers from our company had formed at the glass doors at the entrance. Everyone peered into the darkness in the direction of a hazy orange light on the horizon.

"Something exploded over there." Todd, our oral surgeon, pointed to the distant glow. Two more faraway detonations intensified the orange hue, and then it disappeared.

We waited. For that full minute of silence, every muffled breath I allowed myself to take sounded loudly in my ears. Finally, we dispersed and returned to our rooms, murmuring nervously to one another that it must have been artillery. Jason picked up his computer and placed it in his lap. We both leaned back against the hard concrete wall. Steve and Bill got comfortable again and resumed watching the movie.

The next second, I was jarred to the core. My teeth rattled at the impact. Something splintered against rock and dirt in a tremendous, sickening crack. The concrete walls shuddered, and the windows vibrated violently in their sills. The muscles surrounding my heart gripped it relentlessly in one instant, released it and trembled in the next.

"Flak and Kevlar!" someone bellowed, barely getting the

words out before another staggering impact knocked me away from the cot as I was struggling to stand. My knees buckled and I crumpled to the deck. Jason, Steve, and Bill donned their ballistic body armor, Kevlar helmets, and 9mm pistols.

Crack. The ground quivered again, and although the walls of the concrete structure seemed to waver, they held fast. *Crack.* I instinctually covered the top of my head with my forearms despite the fact that nothing was falling on me. From my hunched position next to Jason's cot, I looked up at him.

"I don't have my flak and Kevlar here," I said. My voice sounded small, unfamiliar, and distant.

Crack. Jason stuffed his ammunition in his cargo pocket. "Come on, I'll go with you to get it."

In the dark, boots thumped through passageways, fists pounded on doors, and voices shouted orders. Officers and senior enlisted men huddled together at the front hatch, talking excitedly. Jason and I moved through them.

The female barracks was one hundred yards away, a straight shot over uneven dirt and rocks. We waited. A full minute passed without an explosion. Jason grabbed my elbow and led me down the stairs.

We ran.

Like the men's building, the passageways of my barracks building were darkened. Jason held out the blue squeeze flashlight that hung from his dog tags and illuminated the combination lock on my door. My fingers quivered so fiercely I was afraid I wouldn't be able to turn the dial. I did, but missed the right numbers. I used every psychological trick in the book to slow my breathing. I found it nearly impossible to practice what I preached.

I got it on the second try. We opened my door and I slid into my flak vest and fastened the chinstrap of my helmet. "Let's go," Jason said, motioning to the group of people who were already running across the field to the hospital.

As I closed the door and replaced the lock, Karen, a junior nurse officer, appeared in the passageway. She was a petite woman, just over five feet tall, but she looked even smaller in her big vest and imposing helmet. Her brown eyes were huge and frightened. I suddenly felt brave. I grabbed her hand.

Jason led the way and the three of us sprinted across the field. I clutched Karen's hand the whole way. Our breathing raced under the adrenaline rush and the thirty pounds of extra weight. We ducked into the front entrance of the hospital, gasping. Our company commander stood in the lobby area and barked for everyone to go to condition one. This weapon configuration, with a magazine inserted and a round in the chamber, had been the one I honestly thought I would never actually use.

I looked at Jason in disbelief. He shrugged, pulled the slide of his pistol back, and chambered a round. Karen and I did the same.

From outside in the cool desert night came the distinct thumping of multiple attack helicopters taking off and turning outbound over the hospital.

• • •

They were rockets. They had been fired toward our base from miles away, and when they struck the dirt and burst into razor-sharp fragments, the resulting crack was astoundingly loud. The rockets also made a bizarre whizzing sound just before contact with the ground, but it took us some time to learn to recognize that. Our deployment changed at the first moment of impact. We became vulnerable in a way that few Americans will ever understand.

By 0330, all incoming casualties had been treated and all medevacs* had departed for Baghdad with our injured patients.

We considered ourselves very fortunate that we hadn't accidentally shot our own comrades that night. It was the first and last time weapons in condition one were allowed inside the hospital.

We were told to return to our barracks and attempt to get some sleep.

The idea of sleep was a joke. I lay wide awake on my cot, too paranoid to permit myself to blink. I listened to the distant shouting of men's voices and the occasional popping of gunfire. Several times during the night, the anxiety overwhelmed me. I got up and knocked on the door next to mine in the barracks, behind which my psychologist colleague and friend Jen was also wide awake. The two of us sat, arms wrapped around each other, shivering, for what seemed like an hour but may have been ten minutes.

---

*Medical evacuation flights.

My heart rate remained elevated, my hands remained frigid, and my eyes remained open during those three cold hours until sunrise. And my thoughts raced. I thought about people in our world who had lived through the horror of being bombed. For the first time in my life, I had a real sense of empathy for them.

I saw a detached image of my own death, even allowing my mind to wander to a mental picture of the car driving up to my house in Florida, and two uniformed officers stepping out. When the vision became too clear, I gulped, squeezed my eyes shut, and forced it away.

I imagined my children and found that, although I could picture them in my mind, I experienced genuine difficulty *feeling* them. I fought to retrieve those tactile memories. After many long moments of searching, I sensed the actual warmth of Meg's tiny body, her little bald head resting on my shoulder. I felt her baby skin smooth against my fingertips. I grew increasingly panic-stricken, however, when a similar sensation of Brian eluded me. I lay completely still and focused on breathing. I battled every external distraction, silencing the sounds of the night and the pounding of my own heart by sheer will, until at last a memory emerged.

The night before I had left for Iraq, Brian suffered a fever and a cough that racked his little body and kept him awake. I had retrieved the coughing baby from his crib and carried him to the couch in the family room. Lying on my back, I rested him on my chest and placed a blanket over both of us. He fell asleep, his face turned sideways over my heart, and the rhythm of his labored breathing synchronized with mine. I stayed awake that entire night watching him.

Tears of relief flooded my eyes. And I knew at that instant I would be unable to function in Iraq if my children stayed at the forefront of my consciousness on a day like today.

In a world where rockets exploded randomly nearby, I decided I could not be a combat psychologist and a mother at the same time. I had to be one or the other.

I had no choice. I put their pictures away.

HOME

My friend Nisha is a redhead, like me. She is also a clinical psychologist in my department in Florida and the mother of · a boy and a girl. And she had deployed to Iraq with the Marines when Captain Goldberg did, in 2003. While our experiences in country turned out to be very different, her words were always a comfort.

An e-mail from her waited for me one morning, one among a large in-box of supportive notes from friends and family. She included updates on our friends and her family, as well as good hospital gossip. Her last paragraph caught me off guard:

> I know this is the most difficult thing you've ever done. I also know a part of you is dying inside, as the days of your children's lives go on without you. I remember the feeling. Fight that. Keep that part of you alive. Listen to the music that feeds your soul. Write in your journal about your grief. Most important of all, find another mom and take turns crying to each other.

I thought of Sandy, the pediatric surgeon whose cot had been next to mine in our tent in Kuwait. Her daughter had just turned two, and although we barely knew each other, we felt immediately connected. We even bought matching stuffed tan camels for our babies and had their names embroidered in Arabic and English at the tailor shop on base.

Then I had come to Alpha Surgical while Sandy went to Bravo, in Fallujah. We had known each other six days. It felt like six years. Leaving her was horrible, and Nisha's e-mail made me realize why.

The people there with me were terrific. Even this early in the deployment, I knew that a handful of them would be some of my most trusted friends for the rest of my life. But the way I would survive would be different from Nisha's.

I did not have another mom out here with whom I could take turns crying.

The Legend of the Camel Spider,
Part I

Since the first day a member of the U.S. military set foot on Middle Eastern sand, the tall tales of the giant prehistoric arachnids who lived there, camouflaged by that same sand, had grown to the size of the spiders themselves. (This was rumored to be roughly equivalent to the diameter of a dessert plate.) But they were not just huge, legend said. These desert monsters sprinted — at ten miles per hour — and had a vertical leap of four feet. And by the time Alpha Surgical Company set up shop in western Iraq, they also had two rows of razor-sharp teeth and growled like rabid wolves before attacking their helpless human prey.

We had been in the hospital less than a month when our first critter casualty appeared. He was a Navy SEAL, a hulk of a man with icy eyes. He was admitted to our medicine ward with a high fever and a nasty cellulitis that spread up and down from the bite on his arm. Before admitting defeat, however, he had captured his nemesis alive.

It was not a camel spider. It was a scorpion. He proudly delivered it to his doctor in an ammo can. Dr. Sladek, our senior medical officer, took one look at the intimidating creature and promptly called the Bug Guy.

The Bug Guy, a Navy entomologist from the preventive medicine unit in country, arrived soon after receiving word about our special warfare Sailor with the sting that was not responding to typical scorpion treatment. The Bug Guy looked into the ammo can and with the giddy excitement of a small child announced, "That's a death stalker!"

Fortunately, he also knew how to treat the sting of the death stalker. After telling the medical staff what to do for the ailing SEAL, he delivered an impromptu Bugs and Snakes lecture for the rest of us.

The eyes of the group of doctors, nurses, and corpsmen who stood around him widened in horror as we heard about what we were up against. It was worse than we thought.

One to 2 percent of the invisible sand flies, the culprits behind the three-week-long episode of excruciating itchy bites that we seemed to suffer every day, carried a serious skin disease called leishmaniasis, the Bug Guy explained.

"The good news," he expanded, "is that they are quite bad at flying, so running a fan at night will keep them grounded."

He also told us that the huge mosquitoes that emerged from our shower drains and swamp cooler vents — impervious to our military-issue repellent — did not carry malaria. This was a good thing, as we had not been issued anti-malaria medication.

He warned us about the cobras, who hid most of the time

but were vicious if cornered, and about the scorpions, the most dangerous of which had stung our SEAL after taking shelter in his sleeping bag.

"Neurotoxic venom," he said. "It's a good thing your patient is as big as he is and that he came in when he did. It could have been a lot worse."

Finally, the Bug Guy described the infamous camel spider, which none of us had yet seen and none of us wanted to see. He explained that, while they were large (the size of a human hand, not a dessert plate) and fast (probably closer to five miles an hour than ten), they could not actually jump very high. He added that they like the shade, and have been known to run alongside a person to stay in his shadow. We looked at each other incredulously, picturing this image, which could not have been more terrifying if it were scripted for an insect horror movie.

"They're aggressive," he said, ending his uplifting talk, "but not poisonous."

Armed with the information about the scorpion and how to treat its stings, Captain Sladek managed to return the SEAL to duty several days later. He was not the last to stay on our ward as a result of the wrath of the death stalker.

That night, I left the hospital late after dealing with a patient in crisis. The crisp night air of the desert spring had faded to a distant memory once summer had arrived, in April. The field between the hospital and the barracks, with its treacherous crevices and large rocks, was devoid of light. I stepped off the cracked sidewalk and reached into my blouse for my dog tags and the squeeze flashlight that hung with them.

At that moment, a loud whoosh in my ear caused me to duck instinctively; I lowered my head to my knees and placed my hands over my scalp. When I dared to look up, my eyes had adjusted to the pitch-black night. I focused on the field ahead of me.

They were vampire bats. At least fifty of them dove and swooped through the night air, tiny black fighter jets in a wild dogfight.

I watched them in disbelief and partial amusement. Of course there were bats here, I mused. And of course they were diving at my head while I walked to my barracks at night. Checking inside my boots every morning for potentially deadly scorpions was simply not enough.

The Eye in the Sky

My watch alarm beeped softly at 0420. I sat straight up and turned it off. I did not feel awake but slept so lightly most of the time that I never felt truly asleep either. In four minutes flat I stumbled out of my cot, added socks and tennis shoes to the olive green T-shirt and matching workout shorts I wore to sleep, brushed my teeth with bottled water, and navigated through the black passageways out the back door of my barracks. I stood in the darkness for a moment, looking for the signal from Bill in the distance: a flashing blue beam from his little squeeze flashlight.

He was there. I carefully moved over the uneven field that separated the men's and women's barracks, lighting the ground beneath my feet before I stepped. Together we traversed to the paved road and began the three-quarter-mile hike to the gym. That 0430 brisk walk was one of my favorite activities of the day. It was very quiet, relatively cool (low 100s), and we had yet to experience whatever humor or horror the day would bring.

With so many factors beyond our control in the deployment, cardiovascular workouts became a means to control one small piece of our lives. Depending on duty schedules and how much sleep we had had the night before, Bill, Karen, Katie, Jason, and I rotated who went each morning. Almost always, Bill and I remained the constant members of our insane early-morning workout club.

Watching the scarlet sun peek above the flat, brown horizon was a highlight of our ridiculous morning routine. Despite the chaos that might occur between the two, both sunrise and sunset in Iraq usually took our breath away with their beauty. That particular morning in late March, Bill and I watched the sunrise with new interest. As the ruby streaks spread across the sky and brightened the edge of our world, they silhouetted a strange object. We stared.

It was a giant blimp-shaped gray balloon. Tethered to the ground by a long rope, it hovered there, close to the headquarters buildings, simultaneously ominous and comforting. We had no idea what it was but figured it had to be important.

We came to call it the Eye in the Sky, because its duty, we learned, was to observe our base and the area surrounding it with sophisticated equipment that sent real-time signals to the Marines who needed to know these things. Of course, its true capability was secret and the source of only rumors for the likes of us, but what we did know was that the Eye in the Sky watched over us, day and night. Some speculated that the new surveillance came to us in the wake of the increased rocket attacks and casualties as the situation in Fallujah deteriorated. We did not care about the reason. We were happy to have it near.

The presence of the little dirigible led to loud, off-key group singing of the Alan Parsons Project song of the same name: "I am the Eye in the Sky, looking at you-oo-oo, I can read your mind . . ." This, of course, always caused fits of hysterical giggling.

Giggling was good. So the Eye in the Sky was good. And after it went up, the rocket attacks subsided for a few weeks. So the Eye in the Sky was *great*.

One morning a few weeks after the Eye appeared, Karen and I walked back from the gym together. It was 0610, and the April sun was warming up fast.

A very junior nurse corps officer, Karen had volunteered to come to Iraq. She told me she had joined the Navy specifically to take care of our Marines in combat and that she saw this deployment as a unique opportunity for the nursing experience of a lifetime. Her expectations had been met, and by April, she had made a career decision. Watching our nurse anesthetists in action, she knew her calling was to go on to graduate school and follow in their footsteps. Whether those footsteps would keep her in the Navy remained to be seen.

We chatted about our families, Karen telling me that her father was the fire chief in the New Jersey town where she'd grown up. Looking at her as she spoke, I suddenly sucked in my breath at the sight that unfolded in my peripheral vision.

A wall of sand was speeding toward us.

In the movie *The Mummy*, the sand rises up as a huge, angry face, chasing after the protagonists and threatening to swallow them whole as they race across the desert. It was like that, only without the gigantic gaping mouth. Karen noticed my expression and followed my gaze just in time to know she needed to turn her back — as I did — to the sand. We bent at our waists and scrunched our eyes shut. The sand struck us as we turned, a blast of pelting rocks and dirt in a gust of wind strong enough to knock us over if we had not been holding on to each other for support. It lasted five seconds and disappeared while our eyes were shut.

We stood up and looked at each other.

"Ow," Karen said, gently touching the back of her leg. "I think a layer of my skin is gone."

"Three of my best friends in the Navy are dermatologists now." I smiled. "One of them, Mary, sent me a card joking that after my deployment I would have no need for microdermabrasion. I'll have to tell her now I understand what she meant."

Karen grinned, wincing a little.

That little burst of sand was a taste of things to come, as springtime in Iraq brought with it one of the most feared parts of deployment to the Middle East: the sandstorm.

In the weeks that followed, these periodic squalls of sand descended on our base in howling fits, like screaming trapped animals. Visibility was so poor I sometimes could not see my hand in front of my face. But unlike our short-lived dust-devil

experience walking back from the gym, the actual storms lasted hours, or days. The sky turned brown, and then orange, and then red. Legend says that in some areas, it turns black. Thankfully, we never got past red.

All this gusting sand meant the Eye in the Sky had to come down, of course. If the wind got too strong, it might blow away.

One night in the middle of one of the sandstorms, I fell asleep with the pathetic cry of the wind rattling my window and whistling through the roof of our building. It had been a twelve-hour day of seeing patients, including being called back to the hospital in the evening to deal with a staff personality issue. Sometimes physical exhaustion trumps all external sensation. I turned on Norah Jones in my headphones and fell asleep in seconds.

Long before dawn, I slid into a vivid dream of driving in an open Humvee on base with Jason and Tom, our surgical company's OB-GYN. The azure sky was clear, and the sun felt balmy. I turned my face upward to enjoy the sensations. As we drove, the Eye in the Sky hovered nearby. We drove close to the small zeppelin, looking up at it and singing our ridiculous song.

As we drove past its tether point, a huge black machine gun — old-fashioned, with cylindrical barrels — emerged from the Eye in the Sky and started shooting at us.

Tom, who was driving, immediately began to swerve violently and sped up to get us out of harm's way. I searched in vain for my helmet (which in reality I would be wearing in a Humvee), finally resorting to covering my head with my arms, screaming in fear as we zigzagged away.

I awoke with a start, sitting straight up and swinging my legs over the side of my cot almost reflexively. My breath caught in my throat and my heart raced.

I reached for my watch on the floor next to my cot: 0345. The night was deathly silent, in contrast to the howling winds of the day before. I peeked out my window through the sandbags and saw stars in the black sky for the first time in days. The sandstorm had passed. We could go back to the gym. I decided I might as well stay awake for the next half hour before I met Bill. I strapped on my headlamp and wrote in my journal about the dream.

Since the storms had passed and the winds subsided, Bill and I expected to see the Eye in the Sky the next day as we walked back from our workout. When it didn't reappear, the rumors immediately began to circulate. My favorite involved the Eye being left up too long and blowing away in a gust of wind, getting stuck on the rooftop of a home in the friendly town right outside our base. The story went on to say that a Marine major had gone into this town looking for the Eye, and when he found it, he paid a couple of Iraqi guys twenty U.S. dollars to guard it for him while he went to get a truck. When he returned, the two guys were still standing there, watching it. Another rumor stated that other people needed the Eye more than we did at that moment.

We would never know. We did know that in the next few days, rockets rained on our base again.

Jason and I spent a great deal of time together. We ate breakfast and lunch together almost every day and talked in the clinic between patients. In the short time we had been together in Iraq, I came to consider him a friend and confidant. He offered clinical insight about my patients that was refreshing and usually very helpful. Most important, I felt safe expressing my own vulnerability and fear to him. So our conversations about patients and the most effective ways to proceed in their treatment often ended in discussion about how the cases affected us and how our own feelings affected our abilities as providers. Freud called this countertransference, and he believed it was a major factor in therapy. Jason believed in Freud.

One of the best aspects of being partners with a psychiatrist who had a Freudian perspective was his comfort with classical dream analysis, something far beyond the purview of my own cognitive-behavioral training. We talked at length about my Eye in the Sky dream, and I learned from Jason that the emotion that woke me out of the defensive cover of sleep was, of course, fear. Fear that the protector could become the enemy.

Or, perhaps more likely, fear of exactly what ended up being true. Fear that the illusion of safety was just that — an illusion, and nothing more.

Karen's Boots

Sunday was the only day I slept in at all, usually until just before Mass, at 0900. One Sunday morning, though, when Karen knocked at 0730, I was wide awake, attempting to unstick my sweaty legs from the top of my vinyl sleeping bag. I yelled for her to come in. She sat on the edge of my cot near my feet as I folded my thin pillow into thirds and propped myself up to look at her.

Her tanned face appeared unusually pale.

"How was last night?" I asked, clearing my throat and tucking a strand of sweaty hair behind my ear.

She did not speak for a long moment, looking away from me as if entranced by something. I waited.

"Pretty brutal," she said finally. "We had two come in from Al Qa'im at about 0300. One was critical."

"What happened?"

She inhaled deeply. "He had a pretty serious abdominal wound and lots of extremity damage. His pressure was bottoming out, and he was bleeding all over the deck of the SST."

We referred to the people of our Shock Stabilization Team and to the trauma bay in which they worked as the SST. The blood of our injured patients was not foreign to the deck of the SST.

"We took him to the OR, and we stabilized him for a little while, but then he started bleeding out . . . the exit wound was huge. We couldn't give him blood fast enough. We went through a lot of units. We couldn't get a pulse or a pressure for what seemed like forever. Finally, Commander V. called it.

"Everybody was wasted. It seemed like everyone wanted to cry, but no one could." I nodded in empathy.

"There was blood all over the OR, and we needed to take a break before we even thought about cleaning it up. So they all left, except me. I sat there for a while, holding his hand, and for some reason I started thinking about his mom, and how sometime today in the States, a Marine would be coming to her door to tell her. I thought of my mom, I just kept seeing her face, and for some reason I started thinking about a Navy chaplain coming to our family's door to tell her. I sat there and cried for a while by myself. Then one of my corpsmen popped his head in, and said, 'Ma'am, the other Marine . . . he's asking for you.'

"I went in to see him. He was still lying there in the SST, about to be moved to the ward."

Karen looked up, still avoiding my eyes, her lips trembling a little. I placed my hand on top of hers.

"He saw me and he said, 'Ma'am, I'm just wondering if you could tell me how my buddy is doing.' " Her voice shuddered.

"I didn't know what to do, so I decided to tell him the truth. I walked over to him, I took his hand, and I shook my head. I told him that his friend wasn't going to be okay. I told him we really tried.

"He started crying then, and I held his hand and we cried together for a little while. I tried to stand at an angle where he couldn't see my boots, but he did. He said, 'Ma'am, is that my friend's blood on your boots?' I thought about lying, but I couldn't. I just nodded yes.

"All he said was, 'Thank you, ma'am, for taking care of my Marine.' "

Karen shut her eyes then. One big tear escaped down her cheek and she raised her forearm to swipe it away. I squeezed her other hand.

She sighed, lowered her head, and said, "So . . . do you know how to get blood off of boots?"

"I've heard hydrogen peroxide works." I swung my legs over the side of my cot. "Come on, I'll help you."

HOME

My father's daily messages continued to fill my e-mail in-box. During my time at the Internet café, I allowed myself a rare indulgence through his words: brief immersion into images of my children's lives. It lasted — at the very most — thirty minutes, at the end of which the Marines who monitored computer use bellowed the words, "Kraft! Your time is up."

It's now 11 pm, and I hear the faint murmurs of our sick babies. It has been a long day. I went to get Pedialyte very early and Meg has kept it down most of the day, but little else. She spent most of the day in your mom's arms. Whenever she cries, I do my best to keep her distracted — I dance, and point to stars, or trees, or birds or planes, or ants. It works for a while.

Brian also woke up with a fever. We gave him Motrin and rocked him, until he went down for a nap at 0930 and slept for four hours. The afternoon was better, but he still seemed sluggish, and not at all himself. Then Mike came home, and both babies could not have been happier. They even waved bye-bye to us as he put them to bed.

I'd best put my head down now, since we have to be ready to assume our duties again early when Mike leaves for work. And I'm tired.

My heart tumbled in my chest. It is really difficult to care for sick children. I felt genuine empathy for Mike and for my parents. I knew I needed to call, to summon the internal strength to provide support for them. I never used to hesitate when someone I loved needed me. Somehow, before Iraq, I was able to be there for my patients and my family and friends, if necessary, with emotional muscle to spare. Today, concrete encased my boots as I stood up and trudged ahead, moving by sheer will into the line for the phone.

"Hi! How is everyone doing?" I tried to sound cheerful.

"Hi." Mike sounded frustrated. "They're both sick, again."

"Yes, I saw my dad's e-mail. I'm so sorry . . . this must be so hard on you." There was a significant delay on our phone connections, so I waited in case he was about to speak. He wasn't. His exhaustion was palpable.

"I suppose it's to be expected," I went on, trying to fill the silence. "Since they've only just started day care a few months ago, they're suddenly being exposed to everything."

"I know." Even across the world, I could sense his stress.

"I'm just so sorry." I didn't know what else to say, so I stopped talking, figuring he needed to vent.

I pursed my lips when they trembled. I didn't want Mike to know how difficult it was for me to hear about his exasperation and my children's illness when I was helpless to intervene. I sunk deeper and deeper into my grief. I knew he was sinking too.

"Kraft! Time's up."

Dunham

Mass casualty. The two words hammered away at us, beginning that first day when we sat together on bleachers at Camp Pendleton, holding our empty seabags in our arms. *Mass casualty.* The words assaulted us after dark during those seven months in the desert. They shattered the nights of silence after we had collapsed onto our hard cots. We wondered each night if sleep would be interrupted by the echo of those two words yelled down the concrete corridors of our barracks. When they came, they catapulted us into strange, trancelike nights that blurred the boundaries between nightmare and reality, helicopters whirring overhead and voices piercing the blackness. The two words even greeted us in the morning as we debriefed the evening's experiences at staff meetings and medical rounds. We talked about the mass casualty, planned for it, ran drills pretending it was happening, and set up elaborate scenarios to make sure we would be able to function when we were totally overwhelmed. With two operating rooms, it did not take much. Any more than two surgical cases exceeded our limited field capacity.

One day in mid-April, nightmare became reality. Although

our experiences to date with multiple patients at once had been called mass casualties, the term was redefined that day.

Right before lunch, I stood in front of the hospital in my flak jacket and helmet, taking a picture of one of my colleagues next to the sandbags and the ALPHA SURGICAL COMPANY red Marine Corps guidon. Chief Edmonson walked outside and approached me as I tucked the camera into the large cargo pocket in my pants. She whispered in my ear, "Don't leave, Doc," as she eyed unsuspecting Marines walking up to the hospital for routine medical or dental care.

"You mean for lunch?" I asked, surprised.

She nodded. "This isn't for sure yet, but we may be getting fourteen from Al Qa'im."

I followed her inside. No sooner had I taken off my helmet than the distant thumping of a Black Hawk's blades beat the desert air, audible even when they were several miles from the hospital. I swallowed and found the back of my throat had risen to form a hard lump.

Minutes later, the helicopters landed on our makeshift pad, one after the other, in a surreal moving image of black fuselage paint and blood red crosses, setting down within huge tornadoes of tan dust. We waited inside, watching through the dirty glass doors, as medical corpsmen and Marines formed into groups of six to carry gurneys.

Dave, our OR nurse and a former Army Special Forces medic, coordinated litter bearers. His voice was low and raspy from too many years of smoking, and as he called their numbers, the teams ducked their heads and ran out to the birds.

KATIE FOSTER SAYBOLT

One by one, each group of six men and women grasped the handles of the gurney, slid it out of the hatch of the Black Hawk, pivoted slowly, and brought the heavy, bandaged, and bleeding patient back inside our hospital.

The corporal was brought in first. I drew in my breath as I saw him. The tube down his throat protruded awkwardly from his mouth. At his brief visit to a forward resuscitative surgical suite before he came to us, other medical personnel had placed this lifesaving artificial airway and applied what was now a blood-soaked bandage around his head. His eyes were shut, bulging from his face and giving his eyelids the appearance of swollen, bruised globes. His name, written in black ink on his bare chest, was Dunham.

His litter team took him to the SST first, and behind him

other teams carried thirteen other patients through the doors according to their triage priority. They formed a crooked line of gurneys resting on the dusty tile floor, each with its litter bearers waiting to pick up their patients again and move them forward in line. Jess, a pediatric cardiologist, and his team of corpsmen worked fast on Corporal Dunham, who had two obvious entrance wounds to the frontal lobes of his brain. The Marine made no meaningful movement, and Jess gave the order that he be moved to the expectant ward. This is the combat medical term for the triage area where casualties who are too critically injured to be saved are placed. Most American doctors, even those with wartime experience, never become used to giving that order. I am not sure Jess ever truly recovered from it.

Our expectant ward appeared to have once been an old laundry room. Its cracking tiled floor surrounded a drain in the center of the room. Even a nonmedical person could figure out why we used that space. Here a patient could be moved away from the chaos of other casualties. Here he could receive pain medication and supportive care until he died.

Our mass casualty plan assigned dentists and dental technicians to monitor the expectant ward. When I arrived, they were taking care of Dunham. I entered the room and spent a few minutes with them as they touched the corporal gently and spoke to him in soft voices. His litter rested on the floor, and they sat around him on the tile. Their legs were folded in uncomfortable positions and they shifted often to maintain circulation. At one point, one of our senior dental technicians, DT1 Graham, rose to change the bag of fluids and asked me to take the Marine's hand that he had been holding.

I was immediately drawn to Corporal Dunham; I was unable to leave him. We told him that we were proud of him and that the Marine Corps was proud of him. The chaplain came in and we all bowed our heads as he prayed out loud, asking God to take this brave Marine into His arms. DT1 Graham went through the front pocket of the Marine's desert utility blouse, which had been cut off and was stuffed behind his head on the gurney. We found the Rules of Engagement card for Operation Iraqi Freedom, which included some basic Arabic words for phrases like *Stop* and *I am an American*. He also carried a small, laminated map of Iraq. His dog tag no longer hung around his neck, likely a result of the blast that injured him. But as regulations required of all of us, his second tag was laced into his boot.

We learned his first two initials were *J.L.* and that he was Methodist. We guessed his first name might be John, or Justin, or Jason. He was not wearing a wedding ring. In combat, that did not mean much, but we pretended it did.

We called him Corporal Dunham as much as possible. We told him he was doing great. We waited, anticipating that his breathing would become labored and his heart rate would become irregular.

They never did. His breathing remained steady and slow, and his heart beat on. Sometimes I swore I could see it moving under the muscles of his chest.

Many long minutes later, I moved his arm. It had looked

uncomfortable to me. He was a tall, muscular young man, and his elbow hung off the edge of the cot. I told him what we were doing, and together DT1 Graham and I picked up his arm and moved it closer to him, adjusting the straps that kept him balanced there. I continued to hold his hand, and as we moved his arm, I felt a distinct squeeze. He had squeezed a few times before, but only in short, reflexive twitches. This was different. His whole biceps muscle flexed as he squeezed. I looked at my colleagues. We didn't breathe. He squeezed again, so hard that he pulled me toward him.

"Corporal Dunham," I said urgently in his ear. "Can you hear me? If you can hear me, squeeze my hand again — now."

He did.

I looked up, making eye contact with DT1 Graham, DT3 Stirling, who was sitting across from me, and James, one of our dentists, who was standing in the corner. Everyone's eyes looked the same: huge and hopeful. I looked at our company commander, who was lingering by the door. She ran for help.

The five physicians of the company arrived at the expectant ward in about one minute flat. Two stethoscopes were placed on his chest, and Mike, a family medicine doctor, looked up and said, "I've got seventy-two beats per minute . . . sounds good to me." Jess held open the Marine's eyelid and flipped a light back and forth. Dunham moved his head in response and squeezed my hand again. Several of us cheered. "Get him out of here" came a shout from somewhere in the room.

Everything sprang into motion. Voices yelled for a litter

team, and within moments their boots pounded down the passageway. They lifted the gurney and moved it into the intensive care unit while the admin clerk called for an urgent surgical medevac. Karen, one of two nurses in the ICU that day, knew that he had been responding to my voice, and in a gesture of friendship I will never forget, she handed me surgical gloves and asked me to continue to hold his hand. He squeezed frequently then, maintaining a strong grip, especially when I told him he was going in a helicopter. I told him my friend Steve, one of our physician assistants and a former helicopter air crewman, would be going with him. I laughed out loud each time he squeezed. He moved his head and feet on command. The energy in the room was electric, and we could not help grinning hopefully at each other. The chaplain wandered back in, looking confused. I told him, laughing, that I thought this young man might need a different prayer.

We heard the roar of the Black Hawk landing outside. The ICU team strapped Corporal Dunham to the gurney, and six litter bearers took its handles, a seventh lifting his IV bag. I kept holding his hand. Steve started hand-ventilating him then, and we all moved into the passageway. It seemed that every person in the company lined those walls as we walked through them and out the double doors. I gripped Dunham's hand tightly and kept talking, unable to control the manic hope in my voice. I told him the doctors and nurses at his next stop would take good care of him, that we would never forget him, and that I was proud of him for fighting so hard. We walked all the way to the helicopter. The Army flight medic met us at the hatch. He motioned the litter bearers to the holding rack.

And then I had to let him go.

The litter team loaded him in the bird, and we all ducked under the vortex of the rotor blades and backed away. The Black Hawk took off. I stood paralyzed in the light brown dirt, watching the cloud of dust rise and the huge propeller lift them to the bright blue horizon. The Black Hawk was joined by an attack escort, and together they made a wide, circling turn over us and disappeared. I turned around. A large group of people had gathered around the back doors and stood in quiet awe. The rest of our patients were either in surgery or on the ward. We could stop for a moment.

I was suddenly aware of my body violently trembling at my knees. I raised shaky hands to my face without realizing I still had my gloves on. And then the tears came.

Combat Action Ribbon

"There are five thousand Marines at Al Taqqadum with no mental health support. I need you to take a psych tech and go down there. Assess the need, talk to the docs, and set up a system so these Marines are covered."

"I see. And when do you need me to do this, sir?"

"Tonight. With me. Convoy leaves at 0200."

The commanding officer of our medical battalion spun on the heel of his boot and strode away without waiting for my reply.

It was April. Fallujah was burning, and the Marines' siege of the city was splashed across front pages around the world. Surgical companies and the smaller forward surgical units — like the one at Al Taqqadum (which we called TQ) — were overwhelmed with casualties. We were no exception.

I watched him walk away, incredulous that he had not been briefed on the fourteen injured patients our group had treated that day. And then I realized the truth. Someone *had* briefed him. Although it must have been clear to him for weeks that a mistake in medical planning made reassignment of psych resources necessary, the CO had decided to sum it up in a three-sentence order to me on the afternoon of our worst mass casualty to date.

The convoy would take us through Hit, a hostile town just south of our base. We had been informed by our Marines that fighting was ongoing in Hit, and there was a possibility of another wave of wounded Marines from the area within hours.

Adrenaline shot through my body, sending a prickly sensation to my toes and fingers. The windows in our concrete hospital structure rattled fiercely as a huge Marine transport helicopter hovered above us, waiting to land. The volume made communication without yelling impossible. I watched as Marines and Sailors formed litter teams and waited inside the glass doors for the signal to go.

The first group ducked their heads and ran to the bird. The noise intensified with the open hatch, so I got earplugs from the tiny pocket on my shoulder and stuffed them in my ears. Watching from the window, I saw the gurneys stacked high inside the helo. The adrenaline rush turned to anger.

I marched down the short hallway between the casualty receiving area and our company commander's office and knocked loudly on her door. No more than five feet tall, the Navy laboratory officer in command of our company wore pink blush and lipstick nearly every day. It may have been the only trace of the color pink in all of Iraq.

At five-eight in my boots, I towered over her and had to look down to make eye contact. She looked up at me. I calmly asked her about the unnecessary risk of a convoy for Petty Officer Blythe and me in this clearly nonemergent situation. I reminded her that we expected numerous additional casualties today and that we were located on an air base. We could hitch a forty-five-minute helicopter hop to TQ twice a day any day of the week. She agreed to talk to the CO.

Less than one hour later, she sent for me and explained that the Marines would not take me on a convoy if they thought it was dangerous. To this day I think that may have been the most ridiculous statement I have ever heard.

I told Jason, Bill, and Steve about my convoy that night, certain that my eyes betrayed my anxiety. For most of our seven months at Al Asad, the four of us ate only breakfast and lunch in the chow hall. The walk was long, and the lines at dinner were longer. Despite this, the three men who would become my dear friends suggested we go to dinner together that night.

Bill and Steve were the physician assistants of our company. Both had been in the Navy for many years, rising to the rank of Navy Chief. They had both been independent-duty corpsmen, responsible for the health of Sailors in situations when physicians were not available. They teamed up with Jason early on as roommates, and their combined vast deployment experience led to important quality-of-life projects, from which I directly benefited. Like the decision early on that we would watch the entire series of *The Sopranos,* and we would make it last the whole deployment. It was something to look forward to; it mattered. They knew it.

Best of all, though, they made me laugh. Their experiences

had given them the wisdom to see the humor in situations that might not have seemed funny at all to someone like me, who didn't know better. We laughed a lot together.

And that night, together, we braved the crowds of thousands of hungry Marines and trudged the half mile to the warehouse turned chow hall. As we approached the two long lines leading to the entrance, Bill ran up to the front to check the menu. He walked back to us with a huge grin on his face. The "express" line boasted corn dogs that night. This was a wonderful surprise, as we had grown to truly love these corn dogs. We grinned at each other like delighted children in the lunch line.

Conversation was sparse during the meal. I knew my friends were angry at the CO and company commander for their collective decision. I knew they were concerned for my safety. Most of all, I knew they felt frustrated that they could not protect me that night.

After dinner, I proceeded to my room and shoved bare necessities into my Marine Corps–issued backpack, called an ALICE pack. Suddenly inspired, I wrote six letters. One of them was to Mike.

I want you to know that, nearly five years ago, you were my dream-come-true when I walked down that aisle and saw you up there in your dress blues. And then sixteen months ago, two more dreams-come-true entered our lives and looked up at us with big blue eyes. No matter what happens tonight or any night out here, my life is complete. I am a lucky woman. All my dreams have come true.

I addressed the cards, placed them in a neat stack on the edge of my cot, and returned to the guys' barracks to watch a movie.

Jason lent me his cushioned stadium seat for the long Humvee ride. He said it had served him well in his deployment to Iraq with the Marines in 2003, and he hoped it would help make me slightly more comfortable. I smiled at him, touched by the gesture. All three of them hovered around me. I felt their worry intensely.

But no one knew what to say. So no one said a word.

Just after midnight, the movie long over, I sat on my cot alone, cleaning my weapon by the light of my headlamp. My fingers trembled, and the twisting sensation in my gut felt the same as it had during the first rocket attack. It was fear, of course, but that night I refused to name it.

Petty Officer Blythe knocked on my door at 0100, his AL-ICE pack over his shoulders. His blue eyes twinkled, and he smiled easily at me. Thankful for his company, I hoisted my pack, and without a word we walked out of my barracks and up the road to the staging area behind the hospital.

A twenty-five-vehicle convoy waited for us around the corner.

The CO met us, we exchanged pleasantries, and then he left to talk to higher-ranking people. His driver, a tall, lanky lance corporal with a Texas accent, helped us load our bags in the back of the Humvee. I noticed the canvas sides of our vehicle and mentally compared them to the armored plates on those in front of and behind us. I was opening my mouth to ask our driver about it when he swung the door of the vehicle open for me, wiggling its metal handle in demonstration.

"Here's your hatch, ma'am," the Marine said. "It's kind of stuck, see? It doesn't open from the inside, so you'll have to wait for me to let you out."

"You're kidding, right?"

"No, ma'am."

Before I could ask the next stupid question, a group of five men approached us.

"We heard there were medical people on the ride tonight." We introduced ourselves all around. They were Navy reservists, paramedics in their civilian lives, and now hospital corpsmen who supported Marine convoys. The senior ranking man, a petty officer first class with a dark mustache and bright green eyes, described the situation.

"So, ma'am, here's what's going to happen when we get hit. If the incident occurs in front of you, your driver will move you to the right and we will come forward to care for casualties. We will meet you there and you both can help us out. If the incident is behind you, your driver will stop in place, and when he gives you the okay, if it's safe, you can make your way back to us."

He lost me with the first sentence.

"I beg your pardon. Did you say *when* we get hit?"

"Well, yeah — we're going right through Hit and ending up

only a few miles from Fallujah. It's been pretty bad lately. Wouldn't you say we've taken fire the last five out of six times?"

One of his colleagues nodded. "Sounds about right."

"We have to expect it, ma'am. It's the rule these days, not the exception."

I stopped talking. Despite my increasing panic, I wanted desperately *not* to look like an idiot. I moved away from the conversation and looked up at the vast black night. Millions of flickering stars illuminated the dark canvas, horizon to horizon. While I struggled to slow my shallow breathing and meditate with words of prayer, a single star darted across the sky in a brilliant stream of light. I figured God was trying to tell me that we would be the exception that night. I made a wish.

Our Marine driver was leaning against the front of the vehicle, smoking a cigarette. He saw me and smiled. I managed a weak smile in return and walked over to him.

"Don't worry, ma'am," he said. "I'll take good care of you."

"Oh, I know you will," I replied. That was the truth.

He dropped his cigarette and crushed it under his boot. "It's pretty straightforward, ma'am. Just watch me the whole time. If we have to stop the vehicle, I want you to point your weapon out the window, square your chest with the door, and keep your eyes on me. I'll get out of the vehicle — you don't have to watch anything except me. If I shoot at something, I want you to empty your magazine in the same direction and then hit the deck of the vehicle. Okay?"

"Okay, but if I'm going to end up hitting the deck anyway, why empty my magazine? Why not go to the deck immediately?"

He grinned. "You have to fire your weapon, ma'am, in order to get the Combat Action Ribbon."

"I don't want the Combat Action Ribbon, Lance Corporal."

"Sure you do."

"No, I don't. Read my lips. *Medical.* I don't shoot this thing except when they make me practice at the range. Trust me on this."

"But that's *why* you want the CAR, ma'am. Imagine how awesome it would be for someone like you to have it."

Someone like me. That made me smile.

"Thanks, but no thanks."

"Believe me, if we go through this thing tonight, you'll want it."

I stopped arguing. He might have a point there.

The engines of the convoy grumbled to life. Marines and Sailors fastened helmet chinstraps, shouted last-minute orders, and mounted their vehicles. My friend the lance corporal opened my canvas door for me and smiled. I hoped he did not notice my trembling knees as I stepped forward. I climbed in, closed my eyes, and silently changed my prayer.

Dear God, please don't let me shoot myself or any of the Marines on this convoy tonight. I opened my eyes and slid a round into the chamber.

Convoy

Our long string of desert tan vehicles crawled from the convoy staging area toward the front gate, stopping adjacent to a large, empty field.

The Marines dismounted. Aiming into the darkness, they tested first the big guns and grenade launchers mounted atop the larger trucks, then proceeded in descending order of size. I stood at the edge of the road and watched.

Despite my earplugs, the volume of the huge guns rattled my brain in its skull. My teeth and eyes ached even before hundreds of Marines holding M16 rifles stepped up to the barbed wire and someone yelled, *"Fire!"* Between spattering bursts of rifle fire, I felt increasingly alarmed at the thought of a headache on the convoy. Earlier unease had led me to dehydrate myself on purpose prior to the trip. I knew I would feel cold, uncomfortable, and possibly terrified on this little drive. That knowledge was anxiety provoking enough without the added worry that I might also need to go to the bathroom during those six hours.

A deep voice called for M9s. Everyone carrying a pistol moved to the edge of the field, including me.

I pointed my weapon at the top of one of the tiny hills and, on cue, fired a single shot into the darkness. The Marines and Sailors around me continued firing. I lowered my arm and clicked the safety on. One was enough.

"Load up!" a voice boomed. We did.

Our driver opened my canvas hatch, waited for me to arrange myself on Jason's stadium chair, and slammed it behind me. We made brief eye contact, and he smiled.

The headlights of every vehicle were turned off. I sat motionless against my steel seat, the chill of the dropping temperatures creeping through me. Several minutes passed in the darkness before, one by one, engines turned over. Our driver donned night-vision goggles, or NVGs, and spent a few minutes making adjustments. Relief washed over me as I recalled fond memories of flying in the backseat of the Hornet using NVGs.* They brought the blackest of nights to surreal green life. I murmured a prayer of thanksgiving for superior technology.

The Humvee, it turns out, is built for many things. Passenger safety as we know it is not one; there were no seat belts to be found. Passenger comfort must have been even lower on the list of priorities. As the vehicle hit the first pothole of the night and my teeth slammed together, I realized that Jason's foam cushion would function as the most basic of shock absorbers.

---

*My designation as a flight psychologist in the Navy required that I log flight hours in military aircraft. I was privileged to log many of those hours in high-performance jets, primarily the F/A-18 Hornet, the vast majority with Marine Corps squadrons.

Resting on my thigh, my pistol vibrated with the undulations of the road. We moved through the front gate, one at a time, until the entire convoy was outside the wire.

My grip tightened.

Our vehicles picked up speed in unison. Leaning to my right, I peered over my driver's shoulder. Even driving sixty-five miles per hour, he still maintained that perfect interval between vehicles. I smiled as I replayed our conversation about the Combat Action Ribbon. For Marines, I thought, earning that ribbon was a source of genuine pride, almost a definition of the values for which they stand. Psychologists who care for Marines, especially in combat, needed to comprehend that fact. It helped make sense of many things. My thoughts wandered to my husband, Mike, and I remembered the first time I saw him in his Charlies, the Marine Corps uniform equivalent of a business suit. He was a striking figure at six-four, with massive biceps and gold wings on his chest. My eyes drifted shut.

I finally understand, I thought, speaking to him in the dark.

We sped into the night. An ebony sky extended in every direction, and with each passing mile, new stars appeared. Starlight alone illuminated the road. Shuddering in the cold, I pulled my fleece face cover over my mouth and nose. I briefly considered gloves but decided against them when I imagined how slippery the wool would feel next to my pistol. Slippery was not good.

After the first half hour, I allowed myself to lean my head back, focusing on the muscles in my shoulders, which felt like rubber bands under tension. Had it only been twelve hours since that mass casualty?

I scrunched my eyes shut, willing the tears to stay inside. Distracted by my trepidation about this convoy, I had not allowed myself time to think about Corporal Dunham. Or about that young lance corporal I had met early in the day as he recovered from surgery on our ward. I remembered the tattoos on his arms. One said USMC. And one, he told me, used to say SEMPER FI. After that day's car bomb had taken out most of his forearm, only the *S* and the *E* remained.

I remembered his tears and the way he swiped mercilessly at them. He felt fear. He felt shame that far outweighed the fear. He went on to explain that he had been in Iraq almost two months. This injury would earn him his *third* Purple Heart. He told me he was afraid his luck was about to run out.

He was ashamed to feel afraid.

I remembered struggling to form the words that would normalize this nineteen-year-old man's experience. And, using a therapeutic technique I made up as I went along, I consciously decided to take another path instead. I told him there was nothing normal about three Purple Hearts in two months. I told him there were no feelings that were usual for people in that situation. I told him he was going home. He laid his head on his pillow and sobbed without making a sound. I sat with him a long time.

I thought of my Brian, only seventeen months old. I pictured myself lying in bed when the phone rang in the darkness. I physically experienced that sick, sinking sensation that must invade every mother's heart the moment she hears a shrill ring fracture the night. I thought of that lance corporal's mother. I thought of Corporal Dunham's mother. I bit my lip hard and tasted blood.

The roar of the Humvee's engine changed pitch, whining with the decrease in speed. My eyes flew open and I peered outside.

Through tall, leaning shadows I discerned storefront buildings lining the road. Decrepit and broken, they reminded me of a movie set for an old Western. I remembered our Marines calling the Al Anbar province of Iraq "the Wild, Wild West." Now I knew why.

My driver called back over his shoulder.

"We're in Hit," he yelled, easing on the brake.

A quiver shot through my chest.

The street curved to the right in a half circle around a patch of dirt and a dead tree. The vehicles of our convoy sped up as they rounded the half circle and slowed as they left it. My pulse pounded in my fingertips pressed against the handle of my pistol.

And then, maintaining that perfect interval between vehicles, our convoy stopped — in the middle of the highway.

Our driver dismounted, telling us in a low voice to stay where we were. I remembered his instructions and turned my chest square to the fabric hatch, ensuring that my body armor faced outward. I rested the barrel of my pistol along the edge of the hole in my door.

I watched the lance corporal. He held his rifle at shoulder level, pointing it at the night, moving it slowly back and forth as he gazed through his goggles. I was glad the blackness in front of my eyes was not in front of his.

Our vehicle had stopped beside a small dirt hill, overgrown with desert brush and weeds. Skinny trees peppered the landscape. I squinted past the mound, making out the shadow of a house in the lot behind it, four hundred feet off the road. All the lights were off.

A dog barked in the distance.

My driver froze, his rifle aimed just left of the hill. Moving only my eyes, I focused on his face, waiting for a move from him.

The dog barked again. I heard the distinct crack of a twig under a boot and sucked in my breath. The barrel of my driver's rifle and of the rifles of the other men who stood on the road beside him moved in unison toward the sound. *Oh God*, I thought. *I cannot believe this is about to happen.* I braced myself for an assault of gunfire.

Four or five minutes passed in total silence. My lungs burned with every breath. Each swallow fought with my pounding heart for space to move down my throat. My eyes watered in the cold, dry air.

Suddenly the desert night was shattered by a tremendous boom. I ducked, lowering my helmet below the level of my window. In that same moment, I realized the source of the sound.

They were Cobras, the Marine Corps' awesome attack helicopters. Their big, beautiful rotor blades chopped the air, flooding the night with thunder as they roared overhead. They flew tight circles over our convoy. Limp with relief, I crumpled at the waist, lowered my weapon to my lap, and rested my helmet on the door.

Our driver got back in the vehicle. The truck in front of us pulled away, and he followed. He yelled back at us, "Well, whoever that was out there, they're gone now." He grinned broadly as he looked upward out the windshield at the Cobras.

The muscles along my neck burned as if they'd been seared by an actual flame. I leaned my head so I could see the stars out the window, feeling the wind blast my face. This time I did not reach for my face warmer. My eyes began to water again, streaking my cheeks with cold tears — one after another, in that perfect interval.

The Irishman and the Lightbulb

The tent at Al Taqqadum was pitch-black inside, all hours of the day. The fourteen women who called it home had different schedules, so they had decided that everyone would navigate by flashlight whenever she was inside. My temporary cot was in the middle of the tent, perpendicular to the rest of them, like the crossbar of an *H*. The other women had towels or personal items, including photos of husbands, children, or Navy SEAL boyfriends hanging above their cots. The air conditioner built into the side of the tent forced most of the women to use thick blankets over their sleeping bags at night.

I lived out of my ALICE pack for the ten days I worked at TQ. Nearby, Fallujah was burning, and casualties were flowing too fast for the on-site Surgical Shock Trauma Platoon to keep up with them. Two junior nurses lived in our female officer tent. Maria and Noelle had been in Iraq for only two months, but they walked with the air of experienced critical care nurses. They also walked with the air of chronic sleep deprivation.

The Marines had come and awakened Maria and Noelle at 0200 on my third morning there. In the few days that I had been at TQ, I had seen both of them sleeping whenever they could catch an hour. This particular night, they had not slept for one minute.

After eating breakfast, I returned to the tent. It was 0800, the sun was bright, and the air outside was heating up. Inside, it was cold and dark, a true sensory-deprivation chamber. I fumbled through my pack for the notebook I used when I saw patients. The fabric door at the opposite side of the tent was lifted, allowing a flash of blinding light, and dropped again. Noelle and Maria entered silently. Maria didn't even take off her boots but collapsed on her cot and pulled her blanket over her head. Noelle undressed in the corner of the tent and changed into sweats that said U.S. NAVY on the chest and right leg. She sat on her cot, sighed deeply, and lowered her face into her hands.

I waited.

A few minutes later she came over.

"How are you, Noelle?" I asked quietly.

"We lost one on the table," she replied, obvious fatigue in her voice. "It just sucks to lose one on the table. I hate it."

"Was this a first for you guys?"

"Yeah. Everyone's wasted, but it probably wasn't as much about losing him as it was about the whole last couple of days. It was bad. There are a couple I can't get out of my head, you know?"

"A couple of patients?"

"Yeah. A group of three of them came in, with their corpsman. The captain was dead; he'd been shot, in under one arm and out under the other. I swear, I think that corpsman probably could've used you, Doc. He had been out there, applying pressure under both the captain's arms. I have no idea how long, but it was a long time. He honestly really believed that if he let go, his captain would die. He didn't realize the guy had probably bled out a long time before he came to us. The corpsman just sat there, in the corner, staring into space. He wouldn't even answer our questions."

"Yeah, that might have been a good person for me to see. Is he still here?"

"Nah, they took him back with them at about zero-five this morning."

"Oh."

"Probably best." She started kicking the wooden floor of the tent, looking at her flip-flop-clad feet. "There was another one, though, that came in with them."

I watched her eyes. She avoided eye contact.

"He was a Gunny. Triple amputee. *Triple.* He'd lost one leg below the knee, one at the hip, and one arm below the elbow. He came in with the corpsman and their captain. He was amazing."

She took a deep breath in and exhaled through pursed lips. "Captain M. had to do a rectal on him before we sent him on the helo to Baghdad . . . you know, checking for internal bleeding. He told the Gunny that he was sorry, that he knew he was dealing with enough, but he still had to do it. The

Gunny was cool about it, saying he understood. When the captain was in the middle of the exam, the Gunny yelled out, 'Hey, Doc, don't I at least get a reach-around?' "

I laughed out loud. She smiled. "All of us looked up. We couldn't believe it. Then people starting chuckling and it spread throughout the room. And suddenly we were all cracking up. And the Gunny just had this smile on his face. Can you believe it? They finished his exam right about the time we had several more come in, so we moved him to holding to wait for the helo, and we started working on the others.

"Things were getting pretty tense in there for a while. I guess the look on my face must have been stressed. I was running by him once, getting some supplies, and he said, 'Hey, ma'am —'

"I felt horrible, thinking that he might have needed more morphine and I was so busy I'd missed it. I went over to him and said, 'You okay, Gunny? Do you need anything?' He said, 'I need to ask you something.' I leaned over him.

" 'How many Irishmen does it take to change a lightbulb?' he whispered to me."

Her eyes filled with tears.

"I couldn't believe it. I said, 'What did you just say?' He smiled at me, and he said, 'It's just far too serious in here, ma'am. You guys need to lighten up.'

"He told jokes the entire time we worked in there. It was like a stand-up routine. When the helo landed, and they came to get him, he waved at us with his one arm and gave us a thumbs-up. We all just stood there like idiots and stared at them loading him in. We'd been laughing so hard for the last half hour, and then they shut the hatch, and it was like opening the fucking floodgates," she said. "We all started crying. A few people even fell to their knees." She rubbed her eyes. "I wonder how he is now. Well, anyway, I probably should hit the rack."

She got up and staggered back to her cot, fumbling through the darkness and trying not to wake Maria. She looked back at me. "Thanks for listening, Doc."

"That's what I'm here for. What an amazing story."

"Yeah," Noelle said, lying back on her pillow. "We all sure are lucky that that Gunny came in and took care of us today."

I got up to leave. "Hey, Noelle?" I whispered.

"Yeah?"

"How many?"

"What?"

"How many Irishmen does it take?"

She smiled. "Twenty-one. One to hold the lightbulb and the other twenty to drink till the room starts spinning."

I nodded. "Of course."

Fallen Angel

Every day is Monday in Iraq, we used to say.

Even Good Friday, it seemed, was Monday — although it did end up being my last day at TQ, which was good. My forty-five-minute helicopter flight back "home" to Al Asad was scheduled for the next evening. I decided to attend a Good Friday vigil at the makeshift wooden chapel at TQ. That night, it just seemed the right thing to do.

At least thirty men and women in identical desert utility uniforms crammed into that tiny room, sitting hip to hip on pieces of lumber with makeshift wooden legs. The Protestant chaplain and the Catholic priest held a joint service, trading Scripture readings, sermons, and Communion. A corporal with a guitar sat on a box in the corner. Illuminated only by the light of a single candle, the room smelled of sweat and freshly cut wood. Shadows from the candle danced across the sleep-deprived faces of Marines and Sailors who might have prayed that night for a few moments of quiet amid the mortars and casualties.

I certainly did.

At one point in the service, I lifted my bowed head and caught a glance of Petty Officer Blythe standing in the open doorway. The moment he caught my eye, he gestured for me to follow him. I knew it was urgent.

We ran through the darkness together without saying a word. A waiting ambulance idled near the battalion aid station, and we jumped in the back. The Humvee rumbled through the black night, toward the Surgical Shock Trauma Platoon.

"I just got the call from the SSTP, ma'am," Petty Officer Blythe yelled over the noise of the vehicle. "They said they had an emergency and they needed you ASAP. Sorry."

"No problem," I yelled back.

The Humvee jerked to a halt in front of one of the four surgical tents. We jumped out and waved our thanks to the corpsman who had driven us, then lifted the fabric hatch of the tent and looked inside.

Halogen lights, suspended by a strong, light multipurpose rope we called 550 cord, hung from the metal tent frame over two makeshift operating tables — gurneys on tall legs. Ten or fifteen masked people in bloodstained scrubs moved around the room, keenly aware of one another in the small space. The intense, crowded feeling in the room made sense to me only after a closer look. Standing at the heads of both of the operating tables, wearing surgical masks but not scrubs, two Marines with loaded M16s hovered over wounded enemy prisoners of war (EPWs). One of the SSTP corpsmen met us at the hatch.

"These guys came in from a firefight in Fallujah," he explained. "The three injured Marines in the ward tent next door have no idea these EPWs are here, and we need to keep it that way. They lost a fellow Marine in that battle."

I swallowed hard.

"Petty Officer Blythe said you guys called for me?"

"Oh, you're the shrink."

"Right."

"Yes, ma'am — let me grab the chief."

Blythe and I waited a few minutes, stealing occasional glances into the OR. One of the EPWs began yelling in Arabic and thrashing on the table. The Marine aimed his rifle at the man. One of the nurses added something to the patient's IV, and the thrashing stopped. The Marine lowered his rifle.

"Commander Kraft." The CO of Med Battalion, the man with whom I had taken my convoy, approached me.

"I was the one who asked to have you called. Walk with me." We left the main surgical tents and walked along a dark pathway. After a minute of silence, he stopped and turned to face me.

"I need your help." The CO's face appeared translucent in the moonlight, and dark rings circled his eyes. He clearly had not slept in some time.

"What's up?"

He exhaled. "Okay. Well, today the medical crew here got slammed with multiple incoming wounded Marines, as you know.

"Apparently one of the men had a serious head injury and showed no signs of recovering. When he died, the call was made to MA [Mortuary Affairs]." I nodded.

"MA came and got this kid — I say *kid* because he was eighteen years old. Anyway, they came and got him. And then about an hour later, the chief here at the SSTP got a call. It was the OIC [Officer in charge] of the MA unit. He said to the chief, 'It looks like our fallen angel hasn't fallen.' "

My eyes widened.

"Apparently, MA did their usual processing for about an hour after the Marine arrived and then got the flight surgeon on call to come and officially pronounce the patient dead."

I nodded. We had a similar procedure at Al Asad.

"The flight surgeon got there, and when he felt for a pulse, the Marine's heart was still beating. He had to explain to the MA guys — who had all gathered around the patient by then — that the patient *was* going to die, that his brain had died, but his heart just hadn't given up yet."

"Wow," I breathed.

"Right. So they all sat around the patient, mesmerized, hopeful even — according to the OIC — for many minutes. Until finally he died."

I looked at my boots, closed my eyes for a long second, and allowed myself to exhale the breath I realized I had been holding. I looked back at him.

"Would you go talk to the OIC? The officers at HQ who talked to him say he's sounding pretty upset."

"Sure," I said.

"So — I understand you're leaving tomorrow?"

"Yes, sir. On a Fifty-three.* No more convoys for me."

"You have to admit, though — our convoy was fun." He smirked at me.

"You have a skewed idea of fun, sir."

I spent most of the night looking for the OIC and the men of MA. I spoke briefly to a few of the Marines involved, and they told the same story the CO had related to me, seen through the eyes of young warriors who had allowed themselves to feel hope.

"I really thought he might make it."

"We were all so excited when the doc said he wasn't dead. We really wanted him to be alive."

"It might have been the worst moment of my life, when they pronounced him."

I never did find the OIC that night.

Sometime before dawn, I trudged back through the thick sand to the female officers' tent. I lifted the canvas hatch and ducked inside, illuminating the path to my cot by blue flashlight.

Far away, at the edge of the desert, the sun rose on Holy Saturday. The wave of casualties receded. Good Friday was

---

*CH-53E, a large cargo and personnel transport helicopter flown by the Marine Corps.

over. It would be etched in my memory for years to come as the day of the fallen angel who had not fallen.

Crumpling to my cot, I pulled my sleeping bag around me in the cool darkness. In the distance, a succession of at least ten mortars boomed, shaking the ground. Even they could not keep me awake.

HOME

While I was at TQ, Alli — my best friend from college — visited Mike and the babies in Florida. Her daughter Leilani is six weeks older than my twins. She and I often laughed as we remembered our late-night talks during freshman year in the dorms at UC San Diego. We had actually fantasized back then about our adult lives, and about our future children — who would, of course, be born only weeks apart — exploring, playing, and growing up together.

On Easter Sunday, the day I returned to Al Asad from TQ, an e-mail from Alli awaited me.

> I am just missing you so much. Tears are streaming down my face as I read your e-mail. There is no way to express my gratitude for what you are doing for our country. You have so much support. Yesterday at the post office I had filled out the wrong type of label for priority mail. The postman was ready to send me to the back of the line until he saw it was a FPO AP address. Then he said "Oh . . . anything for our boys, let me help you fill out the right tags." Of course I had to tell him that you weren't a boy.

Leilani and I had the pleasure of spending a few days with your amazing family. I felt so close to you being in your house. The twins and Leilani were great together, like we knew they would be. Megan is so thoughtful. She loves discovering and then picking up very small things to give to Grandma. She is so calm and sweet, stopping to investigate, smell and pick every flower she sees. Brian loved to pick up, shake and throw the larger items, and then turned to give us all a big grin. All three kids took a bath together — we all ended up wet, too.

Heidi, everyone is doing well, but they miss you so much. Mike and I stayed up late talking on Friday night and he is very lonely. He misses talking to his best friend every night. I only tell you this because I want you to know how much you are loved and missed and how we are all counting the days until you come home.

P.S. Tomorrow Leilani's playgroup is having an Easter Egg Hunt. I stuffed 12 plastic eggs tonight with stickers, fruit gummy candies and toys.

P.P.S. Happy Easter.

Hero,
Part I

Catholic Mass in Iraq was a fascinating phenomenon. Each Sunday at 0900, hundreds of young men and women filed into a huge auditorium that Iraqi soldiers had once used as a movie theater. Inside the vast, dark room with its total lack of moving air, they fanned themselves with small hymnals, rested their rifles on the seats in front of them, and bowed their heads. The priest, whose desert tan boots peeked out from under his white vestment, asked God for strength and courage of conviction on their behalf. They sang hymns off-key, with no accompaniment. And they filed out, were blinded by the sudden Middle Eastern sunshine, and went back to work.

Ten days after the people of Alpha Surgical Company met Corporal Jason Dunham, I found myself filing out of Mass, blinking into the bright April day. Chief Tan, our medevac coordinator, waited for me as I shook the priest's hand and laid my hymnal on a table.

"Ma'am, Corporal Dunham died last night at Naval Medical Center Bethesda."

"Oh." I felt my eyes glaze over.

"His parents were there, and the Commandant of the Marine Corps. His parents made the decision to withdraw life support," the Chief went on.

"I see. When did you hear this?"

"Bethesda called this morning. They know we've been following his progress. I wanted you to hear first."

I lowered my head. "Thanks, Chief."

"I'm sorry, ma'am."

I nodded, biting my lip. "Yeah."

Forcing my feet to move, I found my way to a thick concrete bench outside the decrepit movie theater. Behind Marine Corps–issued ballistic sunglasses, I remembered the intense excitement in the air as Corporal Dunham started squeezing my hand that day. I recalled the past week and a half as we tracked his progress from Baghdad, where he had surgery to relieve pressure in his brain, to Germany, where he had a second operation and stayed for almost a week, to Bethesda, where his parents were waiting for him. I even thought of my idealistic fantasy that he would recover fully and someday we would meet him again. I did not know him at all, yet my eyes brimmed with tears for him and for his heartbroken parents. I lowered my lids, and the tears spilled down my cheeks. The stinging sensation was an odd relief. I lowered my face to my hands and wept.

Nearly a week later, I was on the ward late one evening, finishing paperwork for the medevac of a Marine who had escalating manic symptoms, indicating a serious bipolar disorder. Still reeling from a contentious discussion with the patient's

CO, who had mistaken his Marine's mania for "boundless energy" and "outstanding efficiency" and was not happy about losing him, I rested my head on the table in the nurses' station, mentally exhausted.

"Ma'am?" I looked up. Although most personnel in a Marine Corps surgical company, including the commander, are Navy medical personnel, the executive officer is typically a Marine. Ours was First Lieutenant Catalina Kesler, a former staff sergeant who had gone on to college and Officer Candidate School. Cat loved the Marine Corps, and it showed. Our Sailors and Marines would have followed her anywhere. Cat stood in front of me in physical training, or PT, clothing, holding a sheet of paper.

"Hey, Cat," I said. I continually tried to convince her that since we were two of only five female officers in the entire company, we should use first names. This argument is a losing battle with a Marine.

"I was wondering if you'd seen this article on Corporal Dunham, ma'am," Cat said, passing me the sheet. I looked down and saw a black-and-white photo of a Marine kissing the top of a Kevlar helmet that was perched on a rifle stuck in the sand.

It was a story about his unit's memorial service for him. "Thank you for printing this out for me, Cat."

"Ma'am, it appears that Corporal Dunham threw himself on a grenade," Cat went on.

"What?" My tired eyes flew open.

"He placed his helmet over a live grenade and tucked it under his body, according to that story" — her big brown eyes filled with tears — "to save his men. He's been nominated for the Medal of Honor."

My throat swelled and I struggled to swallow. I looked at Cat and knew there was no need to talk. She understood.

We were not the only people inspired by his story. A reporter embedded with Corporal Dunham's unit wrote about it for America to see, and it was printed on the front page of the *Wall Street Journal*. Mike forwarded it to me simply as a piece that touched him, with no idea of our part in it. My reaction to his e-mail was intense relief — because it was in the press, I could finally share my incredible experience with my family and friends. I wrote an e-mail home, telling everyone about our small role in this young man's fight to stay alive and about how honored I felt to have held his hand.

My e-mail had barely reached the States when we had the opportunity to meet the author of the *Wall Street Journal* article, Michael Phillips, as he transitioned through our base on his way home. He had been contracted to write a book about Corporal Dunham.* After learning that the Marine had received care at our hospital, he arranged to meet us. During the interviews he had with everyone who interacted with the corporal, Karen and I told him that we had both written recent narratives home about our experiences with Dunham. Michael asked for copies of them, which we provided, and he promised to be in touch as the book progressed.

*Michael M. Phillips, *The Gift of Valor: A War Story* (New York: Broadway Books, 2005).

HOME

I pushed the Indiglo button on my plastic digital watch. A bright green hue illuminated the numbers 0214. I could not sleep. In the week after I returned from TQ, the Marine colonel who commanded our larger group in Iraq read my assessment of mental health services there. He ordered Alpha Surgical Company to send its junior psychologist and one of the psych techs to TQ. My friend Jen and my convoy partner Petty Officer Blythe had left for TQ that day. I missed Jen dreadfully already and felt horrible about her departure.

I sat up, strapped my headlamp on, grabbed my little Ziploc bag of stationery and a pen, and wrote a letter to my parents.

> It's hard to be the OIC, Dad. I know you remember, and understand. I worry too much about my people and protecting them from unnecessary risk (like the convoy we took to TQ) to really care about the bureaucracy of it all. I guess I'm not cut out to be the Surgeon General.
>
> Seriously, though, I've made an important decision out

here and have run it by Mike, who supports me. I love being in the Navy. I am so proud to serve the United States, and feel like right now I am doing exactly what the mission of Navy Medicine describes. It is an honor and privilege to be part of it — really. The reality is that if I stay in the Navy, I will be sent back here again. It's just the way things are for us (mental health, surgery, ER, anesthesia, and orthopedics) — we are needed here and there aren't enough of us to go around. But I just cannot let that happen. When I get back, I will be submitting Release from Active Duty paperwork. My Bri Baby and Mini Meg come first, for the rest of my life.

Believe me when I say that before I left for Iraq, I struggled with what the future would hold for my family — I have loved the Navy, as you know. But then I arrived here, and coincidental with the first attack on our base (and then several times since then), I realized how precious each day truly feels. I want to be there for my children, for everything, from the moment I get home.

All this being said, I have no regrets about serving on active duty and about deploying with the Marines in this war. I feel a sense of purpose and of being needed here that is much larger than I am, or than I will ever be. I feel a pull by my country to care for its brave children who are now in harm's way. And I've never been more proud of anything I've ever done in my life. I hope that you are proud of me too — and proud that I am here to serve these absolutely amazing young men and women we call the Marines. If you are, I need nothing else in the world.

Cheeseburgers,
Part I

Even at 0900 in late April, daytime in the desert had developed teeth. The members of the Combat Stress Platoon, only four of us now, were already drenched in sweat. We hitched a ride in the back of one of our ambulances, which was clearly not designed for people who sit upright. We balanced on the edges of metal benches as the Humvee lumbered along; it sent a blow straight through our spines to our teeth with each rock we hit.

Our destination was a huge warehouse located in a remote corner of the base, its front hatch camouflaged under green netting. The perimeter fence of the base snaked along a hill of dirt only a few feet from the building, and watchtowers were visible in all directions. Inside, makeshift partitions on concrete floors created haphazard work spaces, and trailers along the side of the warehouse provided portable barracks.

This was Mortuary Affairs.

We had been summoned there to conduct the first of what would be many group interventions during our deployment. The intent of these groups, which are an important element of combat psychology, was to work with units who had shared a common traumatic experience. The hope was that, together, Marines could process the trauma early and avoid later complications.

I grew nervous as I waited for their officer in charge to meet us. Despite my experience with group therapy in my career thus far, I felt like a novice. I was thankful to have Jason with me.

Jason had deployed as the psychiatrist for First Marine Division during their invasion of Iraq, less than one year before. Despite his resentment at returning to Iraq so soon (especially since his wife was due to deliver their first baby in June), he never compromised patient care. Jason is the most empathetic doctor I have ever known. He reminded me every day of the reason I became a psychologist. He still does.

We worked fast to form a circle out of a pile of folding metal chairs in the corner of the room. I chose a chair across the circle from Jason. The Marines of Mortuary Affairs filed in, eyeing each other bashfully with embarrassed smiles. A slight murmur hummed in the room. Jason straightened his rectangular glasses, crossed his boot over his knee, and nodded at me. The Marines responded to his cue and found seats.

"Good morning. I'm Dr. Bennett. These are my colleagues, Dr. Kraft, Petty Officers Gob and Patacsil. We are the Combat Stress Platoon over at Alpha Surgical. Your OIC asked us to come and talk to you today. He told us that things have been really tough for you as a unit recently."

The group sat in total silence.

"When people have been through difficult experiences, sometimes working through them as a group is best," I added. "The hope is that, together, you'll feel able to discuss anything."

"So, the way we'll proceed is to go around the circle, with everyone having the chance to talk. Everything that is said in this room stays in this room. We expect you to wait your turn and treat your colleagues with respect. That's it. Any questions?"

We got more blank looks than a seventh-grade algebra teacher.

"Let's start with what it has been like for you lately. Who would like to start?" Jason asked.

After a few moments of silence, an olive-skinned lance corporal with black hair and huge shoulders raised his hand. Some of his comrades snickered. He glanced at them sideways before speaking in a hushed tone.

"Well, sir . . . I think the big thing here is that all of us have different MOS's [Military Operational Specialties]. I am a jet-engine mechanic. We have truck drivers, comms guys, supply clerks, even aircrew. Our captain is an infantry officer. But not *one* of us is a mortician. So here we are. At first, it didn't seem so bad. But then . . ." He looked around. The giggling stopped.

"Then everything changed. Marines started dying. Last week we processed the bodies of those four American contractors who were burned and hung from that bridge."

I swallowed hard. That event was the catalyst behind the

captain's call to us. We had heard that those bodies had been sent to this base. My heart ached for this group of men, who had had to take care of the bodies four days after those men had been killed.

The lance corporal's eyes filled with tears.

"It sounds like things have been very intense lately," Jason said softly. The big Marine nodded and wiped at his eyes with his sleeve. Jason looked at the thin blond man next to him, who had raised his hand. "Corporal?"

They were a unit of about twenty-five. They worked in twelve-hour duty shifts of six to eight men; each group was on call to drive the Mortuary Affairs truck to recover a body, prepare it for processing, inventory the personal effects, and fill out paperwork. Unlike the hospital staff, who also cared for people who were going to be all right, the MA unit's work was always about death. They felt fatigue, burnout, and genuine concern about their next five months.

I asked the question that started the second rotation of the circle.

"What has been most difficult for you?"

"The nightmares. They're getting worse. Sometimes I wake up in a cold sweat."

"A few nights ago I dreamed that MA was processing me . . . and it scared the shit out of me." Tears crept down the junior Marine's tanned face and his lips trembled. No one laughed.

"Not being able to talk about it with my fiancée," a dark-haired sergeant said. Several others nodded.

"No one wants to hear about what we do over here."

"Even people who love us. They think they do, but they don't."

"It's just too much for people. My friends on the base from my MOS — I see them at chow sometimes. They ask how things are. But as soon as I start to really tell them, they change the subject."

"Other Marines kind of ignore us. Or they laugh at us. I think we make them uncomfortable."

"It's not like we chose this."

"It's like we're all alone out here. On a base with thousands of people."

"Looking at the personal effects of Marines is the worst," a corporal added. "We're supposed to read their letters and look at the pictures they have in their pockets, to inventory them . . ." His voice trailed off. We waited. He shook his head in a silent *no*, and we moved on to the next person.

"Once, I was going through this Marine's pockets, and there was an ultrasound picture in there," a young lance corporal spoke up spontaneously. "An ultrasound picture. He was going to be a dad." His voice cracked and he looked down, twisting his wedding ring.

Several men lowered their heads, and several others pinched at their eyes. I battled my own tears and sinking internal sensation, blinking away memories of sharing ultrasound printouts of my twins with their father. I did not allow myself the image of that Marine's young wife.

I glanced quickly at Jason, concerned about the effect this

discussion might have on him, with his first baby on the way. He seemed fine.

One of the senior men of the group, a staff sergeant, broke the tense mood.

"For me, the worst thing is that I can't eat cheeseburgers anymore. I can't stand the smell."

"Yeah, me too!" several others chimed in, some of them laughing.

"And that pisses me off, Doc, because I really used to love cheeseburgers." Heads around the circle nodded in understanding.

"Other Marines will come home with other problems. I'll come home a fucking vegetarian."

The Marines shared their final comments, one theme emerging again and again.

"They say combat units understand each other like no one else in the world. You know, like *Band of Brothers*."

I had not seen *Band of Brothers*. I made a mental note to do so. Maybe just not out here.

"But in our case it's more than that. This is all we did out here."

"No one else did anything even close to it."

"This is all we did. And we're the only ones who did it. We will have to count on each other and no one else."

"I guess we're all we have."

Light Discipline

The hospital was totally dark.

I trudged through the endless dirt that surrounded the building on all sides, focusing intently on the ground to avoid the deep holes and large rocks in my path. I reached the entrance and extended an arm to open the door.

"Evening, ma'am." A deep voice startled me.

"Oh!" I exhaled. "Good evening, Corporal."

He sat easily in the hard chair just outside the entrance to the building. The Marine's long legs stretched straight in front of him, boots crossed at the ankles and his M16 rifle balanced across his lap. His gray eyes pierced the darkness. I smiled at him.

"Quiet tonight?"

"From where I'm sitting — yes, ma'am."

"Well. That's a good thing."

"Yes, ma'am."

I opened the heavy, hazy glass door, across which a thick strip of silver duct tape covered a large crack. As I stepped in, my boot caught the corner of one of the gurneys stacked in a pile just inside the door. I stumbled, and it crashed loudly to the deck. Pulling my dog tags out of my shirt, I squeezed the tiny blue-beamed flashlight hanging on the chain. The corporal got up to help me put the gurneys back. I grinned at him. "Pretty dark in here, isn't it?"

"Yes, ma'am." White teeth gleamed in the night.

The commanding general of the Marine Aircraft Wing, on whose sprawling base our little field hospital functioned, ordered mandatory light discipline once the rocket attacks started again. Sandbags shrouded every window in the decrepit and cracking concrete facility we occupied, and the various lamps we hauled with us from the States sat unused in the darkness. Red or blue lens covers rendered everyday flashlights nearly useless by normal standards. We had learned about this combat phenomenon called light discipline from our Marines.

I marveled again — as I moved past the front lobby area and navigated the shadowy passageway by my tiny blue beam — how pitch-black and genuinely spooky Iraq could be. This hospital was especially scary with its thick, gray concrete walls crumbling at the edges and cracking at the foundation, allowing a wide variety of undesirables to crawl or fly in through the holes.

The doctors, nurses, and corpsmen who took care of the Iraqi air force worked here not long ago. They performed surgery, assessed trauma, started IVs, and administered morphine, all within the confines of these same deteriorating walls. As our days in Iraq marched on and as our nights in Iraq became blacker and louder, those ghost stories we concocted when we first arrived seemed likely to be true.

I rounded the corner and noticed a hint of blue light peeking under a closed wood door. I knocked quietly.

"Come in," called a loud voice.

I smiled around the door. Bill sat with his feet up on a makeshift table, listening to music.

"Hey-hey!" Bill called in a manner far too jovial for the middle of the night. He removed his iPod earpieces and swung his boots to the deck. "How's it going, Heidi?"

"Dark. Still waiting for my eyes to adjust. How goes the night of duty?"

"Really busy about two hours ago. Three in from Al Qa'im. Tony and Tom just took the last one to the OR. The other two are in the ward, stable. Routine medevacs have been called for them. I'm just standing by now for when the third gets done."

"You hanging in there?"

"Sure. I'll sleep later."

I closed the door to the duty room and moved on.

Finally reaching the wide passageway along the back of the building, I advanced by the blue glow I pointed at the cracking tile deck — recently mopped, but filthy again. I was surprised to see an intense white light ahead, radiating from the open doorway of the medical ward. Alarmed, I called down the hall, not remembering which of my nurse roommates was on duty that night.

"Karen? Katie?"

As I neared the hatch, the silhouette of a tall young man appeared in the blinding light of the doorway. He wore the standard garb of our patients — olive green shorts and an olive green T-shirt. A thick gauze bandage, more red than white, bound his head. He raised an IV bag in his right hand above the level of his heart.

I hurried to reach him.

"Hey, Marine," I called loudly. "What do you need? I'll get your nurse. First, though, let's get these lights off and get you back to bed." I reached out and touched his shoulder. Feeling my touch, he turned to face me.

His swollen eyes — grotesque, purple globes — protruded from his face. A thick red teardrop slid down his blackened cheek. He opened his lids in my direction.

A piercing pain shot through me. I saw straight through his skin, to the end of the darkened hall.

I gasped for a breath that refused to come.

I bolted straight up on my hard, olive green cot, my breathing shallow and fast and my heart thumping relentlessly in my throat. I glanced around at the concrete walls, at the chipped white paint and the hole in one corner of the ceiling. A beam of moonlight peeked over the sandbags outside my window and cast a hazy spotlight on the American flag thumbtacked to my wall.

A helicopter roared over our barracks. I held my breath, waiting to hear it make the base turn to the hospital. It didn't.

The distinctive chop of the blades against the hot desert air faded into the night.

I collapsed against my thin pillow and struggled to remember techniques I had taught to patients with anxiety to help control breathing and slow heart rate. The swamp coolers in our barracks building blew only semicomfortable air into our rooms, making it far too hot for any type of blanket. Better than nothing, I reminded myself, and certainly far superior to anything the Marine infantrymen at the Syrian border had. I counted to ten and inhaled slowly.

I was drenched in the sweat of sleeping, if only for a short time, in a concrete oven in the middle of the desert.

I was drenched in the sweat of the third nightmare in as many nights about a dead Marine.

Friday Night Fights

"Is Cat coming with us to dinner?" I asked Katie, sitting on my cot and extending a leg. I laced my boots, tucked the laces behind the tongue, and folded the edges of my pants under green blousing bands.

"She's at the gym with Sergeant Snow," Katie told me, rummaging through the care package that had arrived for her. She smiled as she pulled out a package of Oreos. "Score."

She stood up, strapped her pistol to her thigh, and grabbed her cover from her cot. "She's training on the bag with him. I guess she's going to fight on Friday."

"I beg your pardon?"

"You haven't heard about Friday Night Fights?"

"Friday night what?"

"Friday Night Fights. One of the squadrons apparently brought this full-size boxing ring out here with them. Cat says it's just like the pros use. So they've finally gotten the green light to use it, and Friday Night Fights are starting this week. They've organized weight categories, refs, intro music — everything. I guess there are twenty fighters signed up al-

ready. Even women! They're going to do it in the big hangar."
She smiled. "You ready to go to chow?"

I blinked. "Sure," I said, grabbing my own floppy cover and
sunglasses and following her out the door.

There were several distinct moments during my long visit
to this strange desert land when I was dramatically struck by
how bizarre an existence we had here. One moment was the
first time I noticed the high-dive platform overlooking the decrepit blue swimming pool near the base exchange. The Marines used it as a water treatment facility. But at that moment,
I had to physically shake my head to clear the bizarre image of
skinny, mustached Iraqi soldiers in swimming trunks climb-
ing up the ladder to that diving board. Another moment was
hearing that a helicopter squadron in the United States Marine Corps had actually packed up a boxing ring and hauled it
around the world to a combat zone.

That was before Friday Night Fights. It took only that first
Friday night to make me realize there was nothing bizarre
about it. The fact that a boxing ring made the trip to Iraq was
actually one of the sanest things to happen in that place.

The hood of one of our ambulances provided the best seats in
the house for the crew that was assigned as medical backup
for the fights. The hangar was a short walk from our barracks,
so a large group from the hospital went to the event together.
Everyone carried the canvas stadium chair he or she had
bought from the exchange early on when it had become obvious there was nowhere to sit in Iraq. We entered the huge

helicopter hangar built into the side of a dirt hill and found a place, among the many hundreds of other men and women, to set up our chairs.

The electricity in the air was palpable. The ring was beautifully illuminated by hanging spotlights. Referees and announcers had been chosen out of the civilian MWR (Morale, Welfare, and Recreation) employees, and they hovered near the ring. There was even a microphone and speaker system. And they worked.

"Ladies and gentlemen . . . welcome to MCAS Al Asad Friday Night Fights!"

The crowd roared.

"In the first category, weighing in this morning at one hundred forty-nine pounds, from Marine Aviation Logistics Squadron, please welcome — Corporal Jiiiiiiim Iveeeeeeey!" A section of the crowd sitting together near the ring cheered, and another group booed loudly. Jason and I grinned at each other. Immediately following the announcer's introduction, music blared over the speaker so loudly I had no idea what song it was. It was a Mötley Crüe tune, Jason informed me. The people in the crowd craned their necks to see Corporal Ivey as he entered the hangar wearing a red groin protector, red padded helmet, and red gloves. Huge tattoos of Japanese characters graced his thin, muscular back. He danced up to the ring with an entourage of people who strode in with him in a long line. One massaged his shoulders, one carried a towel, and another carried a water bottle. Several of them held their arms up with clenched fists in premature victory.

Twelve matches lasted nearly three hours and ended with the heavyweight fight, which was won handily by the hospital's own Sergeant Snow. The voices of our small band of surgical company staff were hoarse by then. Our attempt at a show of force was hindered by the loss of two ambulance drivers, one nurse, and several corpsmen. They had had to leave early with a Marine in one of the middleweight categories who forfeited the fight when his right shoulder was dislocated.

The last fight of the evening was supposed to be the women. Cat won by forfeit when her opponent did not show. The crowd murmured that Cat would have competition next Friday. It was widely rumored that a tough, petite staff sergeant — and mother of two-year-old twin boys — had put her name on the list.

As we folded our chairs and made our way down the short road to the hospital, I surveyed the swarm of Marines around us as they loaded into trucks and Humvees. They grinned and talked loudly as they recalled the best moments of that Friday night's fight — the surprise upsets, the obvious champions — and speculated about the women's match, which would be the highlighted event next week.*

It lasted only five weeks. The general canceled Friday Night Fights when he learned that we had medevaced five Ma-

---

* Cat won that fight and became the uncontested female champion on the base.

rines, one each week, five Fridays in a row, with fight-related injuries.

But those five Fridays brought intense magic to our little corner of Iraq. For three totally enthralling hours each week, we were not Marines and Sailors in a combat zone. We were simply spectators at a boxing match. And with the exception of baseball, it is difficult to find anything more American than boxing.

We had been transported home.

HEIDI KRAFT

HOME

My baby needed surgery.

The placement of tubes to relieve Brian's chronic ear infections constituted minor surgery only, and the pediatric surgeon told Mike the whole thing would last five minutes. But despite intellectually knowing these facts, I ached with the intense sadness of not being there the moment he went under anesthesia and the moment he came out.

Everything about the situation felt wrong. When Mike wrote to tell me the surgery had been scheduled, I felt a powerful need to cry. I willed the tears to come. They refused. During the time I knew Brian was at the hospital, I sat in the dark, dry-eyed and alone.

The phones went down for operational security (OPSEC) reasons that day. (Phones and nonsecret Internet access were shut down after a fatality or a classified incident until next of kin were notified or other operational planning took place.)

They stayed down for nearly a week.

Up the Stairs

"Oscar Four Kilo, this is Echo Five Golf."

"Go ahead," I answered my radio, walking out of the barracks in the direction of the hospital. As always, the brilliant sun blinded me in that first moment outside, despite the protection of the full-coverage sunglasses we were issued.

"Ma'am, the front desk sent a staff sergeant over, a little while ago. He's escorting a patient."

"I'm on my way," I said.

I strode across the field to our office. Intense sandstorms, with howling wind and tiny pelting rocks, had rendered our entire universe a shade of red during the past two days. Now everything nestled under a blanket of fine dirt.

The door to our tiny office was padlocked, and the paper sign hanging on the nail in its center was flipped to the side that said COMBAT STRESS PLATOON . . . AFTER-HOURS EMERGENCIES GO TO MAIN HOSPITAL.

I surveyed the collars of the men milling about nearby for the chevrons of a staff sergeant and for the unmistakable look of annoyance and concern often seen on the face of a staff noncommissioned officer tasked to escort one of his Marines to the shrink.

He found me. "Excuse me, ma'am, are you the doc?"

"That's me. Heidi Kraft." I extended my hand.

"Staff Sergeant Martin."

"What can you tell me?"

"Well, ma'am, Lance Corporal Adams has started worrying people in our shop. She's always been quiet, but for the last few days, she's crying all the time. She won't talk at all, to anyone. She just sits and stares, and cries. She's started not coming to work. She's gotten in trouble, but it's like she doesn't care."

"Has she mentioned to anyone that she might want to hurt herself or anyone else?"

"No, but then again, she really doesn't talk to anyone anymore."

"Okay, thanks. Where is she?" We walked out into the passageway together. He looked around briefly and said, "I guess she's still in the head."

"Still? When did she go up there?" The marginally functional restrooms were upstairs in the theater, where an Iraqi vendor sold bootlegged DVDs for eight U.S. dollars.

"Oh, about thirty minutes ago, I guess."

The words had barely escaped his lips when I was bounding up the stairs by twos. I felt my chest tightening and was aware of my pulse in my throat. "Shit," I breathed to no one in particular. Shit, shit, shit.

I reached the open restroom door. There were two small

stalls inside. One door was closed. A desert utility floppy hat lay upside down on the tile outside of the door. A folded piece of paper rested inside it. I picked up the paper and pounded on the door.

"Lance Corporal Adams?" Nothing. I pounded louder.

"*Lance Corporal Adams?* Are you in there?" Silence. I tried the handle and it was locked. A wave of nausea washed over me as I opened the piece of paper.

I am sorry.

Shit. I pounded again, not exactly sure why.

"Lance Corporal Adams, I am Lieutenant Commander Kraft. I'm a psychologist. I need you to open this door right now. That is an order." I heard a muffled cry beyond the splintered wood door, and the handle turned. I exhaled, realizing I hadn't been breathing.

She sat on the closed toilet seat cover, her knees parted and her head down. Her blond hair was pulled in a tight bun at the nape of her neck. Her hands were wrapped around the barrel of her M16, upon which she rested her forehead. She looked up at me, raising her face away from her weapon and displaying bloodshot blue eyes and swollen red eyelids. Her pale skin was streaked with dust and tears. She stared at me, lips quivering. Fresh tears streamed down her cheeks.

"It's okay," I whispered. Certain she could hear the hammering of my heart, I took a cautious step toward her. Without changing her gaze, she handed her rifle to me in a slow, deliberate movement. I leaned it against the wall and bent over her. "It's going to be okay." I placed my hand under her elbow and helped her to her feet. She sobbed loudly as she stood up, crying out as if breathing were intensely painful. I handed her the note, which she clutched to her chest. I picked up her heavy weapon, and the two of us emerged from the bathroom.

I called my psych tech on the radio and told him in our special code that I was bringing another patient to the ward.

Staff Sergeant Martin waited for us at the exit closest to the hospital. I handed him her rifle as I opened the door for her. She walked out ahead of me, looking at the ground and shuffling her boots in the dirt, kicking up a cloud of fine dust.

I met his eyes. Neither of us spoke a word. He followed me out the door.

For two days, Lance Corporal Adams stayed on our ward. She did not speak a single word the entire time. Her outward emotional presence clearly indicated significant depression, but without her really speaking to us, it was difficult to ascertain anything else about her experience. The only thing clear to me was that my hands were tied. In a normal situation, I would have time to work with her and help her move toward the appropriate treatment. Out here, I knew only one thing: she needed to go home.

At the end of the two days, the lance corporal's unit brought her a small bag of her personal items. She shook my hand, making eye contact for the first time, and together we walked down the passageway, out the back door, and across the field to the medevac helicopter. Jason had started her on an antidepressant medication, but she knew her recovery would also include intensive therapy (which we had arranged) once she returned home. She spoke the only words I heard from her immediately before her departure. She told me she was ready to get better.

I believed her.

As she placed her bag between her boots and the flight medic helped her fasten her seat belt, she peered out the open hatch at me.

I am not sure, but I think I saw the faintest trace of hope in her small smile.

HOME

Jason's baby was on the way within the month, and I hoped to make the day as wonderful as possible out here when his new son arrived. I needed help. I turned to the source. My sister, Stephanie, three years my junior and as different as possible from her older sister in every way, consistently sent the most terrific and thoughtful packages I received. She always included Victoria's Secret pear lotion, so that I could "smell like myself" here. I did not tell her people laughed at me when I smelled like a pear. It didn't even matter. I still loved putting it on once in a while.

I asked Steph to send us a baby shower in a box, complete with balloons, streamers, napkins, plates, candles, a gift bag, a card, and some wonderfully nonperishable Hostess cupcakes. She did. A card accompanied the box.

And you thought you were the only redhead in the family. Last weekend, in my spring fever state of needing to do something wild and different, I decided to dye my hair "dark auburn brown" — but to add extra red highlights, I mixed the box with a box of "sunset red." Need I say more? Unfor-

120

tunately, I did not read the part of the instructions that say "not to be used on blonde hair" and now all the blonde highlights by my face are an interesting shade of purple. Luckily, it washes out in 28 days, but I have to say, I've actually gotten a lot of compliments (out of pity maybe?). Anyway — you are not the only redhead in the family, just the only natural one. Speaking of hair, when you come back through San Diego, do you want to do a beauty day with me? I'll take the day off work — I was thinking we could get our hair cut and have manicures/pedicures. Of course, Mark is still here and you know what an amazing hair designer he is — I'm sure he could have you looking positively normal again in no time.

So strange, the things that made me long for home. Suddenly the thought of a real haircut was the most delicious I had ever experienced. I trudged down the passageway of the barracks to the head, and examined my air-dried hair in a broken piece of mirror propped up against the wall. I tucked a few stringy, sweaty strands behind my ears, put on my floppy hat, and strode out.

One Good Eye

An urgent call crackled through the speaker on my hand-held radio. "Triage request for combat stress." This meant possible cot-side psychological intervention for casualties. When I arrived, I found our sick call area busy, with less seriously wounded patients filling exam rooms and spilling into the passageway. In the center of the activity, Bill looked calm.

"Let's get these guys cleaned up," he told one of the corpsmen, who guided three Marines in bloodstained uniforms to a cleared area in the passageway and seated them on cots. Each had been hit with shrapnel in his arms, legs, or face, but all three of them were walking and talking.

Bill acknowledged me with a smile as he hurried back to an exam room. The power was out across the base and the hospital felt like a sauna, except in the OR, the ward, and the lab, where the backup generators ran the tiny window air-conditioning units. Bill's blouse was off, and sweat darkened his green T-shirt and glistened off the 9mm pistol hanging over his shoulders in a leather holster.

"IED?" I asked.

"Yep."

"Just those three there?"

"No, their sergeant's in here." He motioned toward the open door, hands full of supplies. He lowered his voice and leaned toward me. "He lost his eye in the explosion. The lid is intact, but the eye itself is just gone. Except for this single black rod, which might be the optic nerve."

I followed him into the exam room, where a stocky Marine with dark hair lay on the makeshift table. His slightly deformed left eyelid and superficial lacerations on his cheek and chin would never have suggested that the eye underneath was missing. He moaned as Bill opened his lid with gloved hands.

"You okay, Sergeant?" Bill asked him. "I'm just taking a look here real quick."

"Sure," the patient said quietly, biting his lip.

I drew in my breath when I saw what was under his eyelid. A thin, dark stem of tissue protruded from the gaping empty socket. The Marine would be sent via urgent medevac to Baghdad to see an ophthalmologist. If it involved "life, limb, or eyesight," the helo was here in thirty minutes.

"Amazing, huh?" Bill whispered. I nodded as we looked at each other. Just then the Marine grabbed Bill's wrist.

"Hey, Doc?" he asked.

"What's up, Sergeant?"

"My eye's not going to make it, is it?"

"I'm not going to lie to you, it's not good," Bill answered carefully.

"My mom's going to kill me," the patient joked with a wry grin. Bill and I smiled too.

"Hey, Doc?"

"Yes?"

"Is my other eye okay?"

"It looks that way to me."

"Can I open it?"

"Sure," Bill said. "Let me get something to patch the injured one first, though, okay?" He motioned for one of his corpsmen, who moved in to place gauze and medical tape

MICHAEL PHILLIPS

over the mutilated eye. The Marine asked for help to sit up, opened his intact eye, and scanned the passageway. He recognized the members of his fire team, who by now had their shirts off and were having their wounds dressed. He silently counted them.

He sighed with a smile, and gingerly lowered himself back to the cot.

"Thanks, Doc," he said, closing his eye. "I only have one good eye, but I can see that my Marines are okay."

HOME

I attended Mass on Mother's Day. During the sermon, the priest told the Marines and Sailors in the stifling auditorium that we should be thankful for our mothers and wives today. He said, "There are no mothers here, but if there were, we would ask God to protect them and send them safely home to their children." Standing next to me, Karen exhaled sharply in exasperation and looked at me with big brown eyes. I smiled at her and bowed my head, giving thanks for my own mother and her great sacrifice for her child this Mother's Day.

The lines to call home snaked far from the entrance to the phone tent. I waited.

I talked to my mom for most of my thirty minutes. She described a fantastic day, saying my dad, Mike, and the babies took her to brunch at the golf club. I thanked her for being there and for loving my babies. I told her I was okay and not to worry. I realized how ridiculous that sounded, but I said it anyway. Her voice tightened as she said goodbye and handed the phone to Mike.

Mike told me Brian had recovered perfectly from the

surgery. It really did last only five minutes, he said, and barely two hours after he had been under general anesthesia, Bri Baby was making fish lips on the glass of the hospital's aquarium as they left. They already noticed a remarkable difference in his ability to hear.

Brian's wonderful baby squeals pierced the air as my parents tickled him in the background. Meg, who was sitting in Mike's lap, reached for the phone. As he always did before he hung up, Mike told her to "say bye-bye to Mommy." For the first time, she actually did.

"Bye-bye, Mommy."

Rule Number Two

Jason and I stood together at the front entrance to the hospital, watching as two sand-colored buses pulled up to the curb. The doors opened, and one by one, scores of men and women slowly emerged.

They looked just a little different from most other people on our base. Their uniforms were not the new digital desert utilities worn by the Marine Corps and their Navy medical support personnel but the older tan-and-brown camouflage pattern. The men's haircuts were just a little longer than the Marines', the women's hair pulled back just a little looser. Their hands were rough and tanned. Their faces were etched with the lines of years, and of years working outdoors in the sun.

This was the Naval Mobile Construction Battalion, affectionately known as the Seabees.

Their unit chaplain had come to the Combat Stress Platoon the day before. His eyes brimmed with tears as he begged for our help. Upon hearing the situation, Jason immediately asked our psych techs to cancel our appointments so we could accommodate four groups of fifteen to twenty Sailors each.

It was 0800. The boots of the first group of eighteen Seabees pounded down the concrete steps to the basement of the hospital. The four of us waited for them downstairs in the whitewashed concrete room. Despite the two high-powered fans our Marines had set up for us, the temperature in the room was already intolerable.

I surveyed the Sailors as they took seats around the circle and placed their rifles on the floor. All of their eyes appeared red and swollen. Their heads hung, and their shoulders slumped. Several of them held hands.

"Good morning," Jason started, his voice echoing in the large room. The hum of the fans became the only sound. He introduced us quickly and explained that their chaplain had asked us to meet them today. He turned to me.

"First of all," I said, scanning the circle of fatigued faces, "on behalf of my colleagues — I am so very, very sorry for your tremendous loss."

My words opened floodgates of emotion. Nearly half of the men and women in the circle released loud sobs, several leaning forward to cover their faces with their hands. Others embraced one another and wept. A stoic master chief spoke for the group.

"Thank you, ma'am." His deep voice trembled.

"We realize that your emotion is very acute," Jason spoke over the muffled crying. "We also know that it is very painful to speak of your grief. We appreciate your trust in us to help you move through this time." A few of them looked at him and nodded.

They started talking.

Only four days prior, a group from their battalion had convoyed through western Iraq in support of the Marines' combat engineers. A Humvee in their convoy, carrying four Seabees, hit an IED and exploded. Two of their comrades were killed instantaneously in the blast. Another two were rushed to us at Alpha Surgical. I remembered them. One underwent extensive stabilizing surgery and was medevaced to Baghdad. The other suffered a traumatic brain injury.

"Heidi, this Seabee from the IED attack — can you come over now and see him? I'm worried about a head injury." Karen had rushed over to the barracks from the hospital to find me that day.

"He is not making any sense when he talks," she explained. "But it's like he knows that he's not making sense — because he is getting tears in his eyes trying to tell me something. He made a motion to me like he wanted to write, so I found him a pencil and placed it in his hand. He put it to the paper, eraser-side first. He tried to write but of course nothing happened. He just looked at me with these big eyes, tears streaming down his face. I turned the pencil around for him and tried to smile and be supportive. I told him to take his time. But when he tried to write, he couldn't. He finally gave up, just sat and cried. I sat with him and held his hand for a while."

I had agreed to see him, but even as Karen and I walked to the hospital together, his medevac lifted off. Obviously, our surgeons had agreed with Karen's assessment. He would be seen by the neurologist at Baghdad that same day and likely sent home as soon as possible. It was for the best, I thought. After all, what exactly did I think I would be able to do for him out here?

I shook my head to clear the memory of Karen's description of her patient's pain and of my resulting feelings of frustration and helplessness. I focused again on the Seabees around me. One by one, they went around the circle and told us their stories.

Most of their Seabee reserve unit had been together for over eighteen years. Their average age was thirty-eight. The unit had been divided when they arrived in Iraq. One group set up at Ramadi, a small headquarters base near Fallujah; the other at Al Asad.

The IED attack on their convoy occurred four days ago. The very next day, still reeling from that loss, the Al Asad Seabees received more terrible news.

While the Ramadi Seabees had gathered together in a staging area, enemy mortar shells fell on the compound. Six Sailors were killed and another thirty-two critically injured.

The first group of Al Asad Seabees cried together. They expressed grief, anger, fear, and fatigue. They talked of survivors' guilt. They left the hospital basement that morning emotionally exhausted, some of them physically supporting each other as they climbed the stairs.

As they walked out, another group of sixteen filed in.

For five hours, Jason, Petty Officer Patacsil, Petty Officer Gob, and I stayed in that basement room, our T-shirts stained darker and darker with sweat as each minute passed.

The last group of Seabees climbed back onto their bus. We turned off the fans, closed the doors, and walked out of the basement together. Back in our little office, the four of us opened a box of meals ready-to-eat (MREs) and started trading for our favorites.* I found the cheese tortellini and traded HM2 Gob my Skittles for his M&Ms. We sat quietly, eating our brown-plastic-pouch lunches with our brown plastic spoons.

The techs got up to leave. We thanked them, telling them to take the rest of the day off. We all chuckled.

Jason and I stayed. The miniature wall air-conditioning unit in our office blew frigid air at our faces. We shivered as our sweat-drenched clothing now became overchilled. We sat next to each other on the hard folding chairs we had propped up against the concrete wall.

I looked at Jason. He slumped in his chair, head leaning back against the concrete. His legs stretched straight out in front of him, tan boots crossed at the ankles. His arms dangled to his sides and almost touched the floor. He turned his head and looked at me. My posture must have looked nearly identical to his.

---

*MREs were the combat rations sent to Iraq with the Marines. We ate them more often than not for a period of several weeks when food convoys were not getting to our base due to significant risk to the contractors who drove the trucks.

"How ya doing?" he slurred good-naturedly. I managed a weak smile.

"I feel like I've been hit by a Mack truck," I stated simply. It was true. My entire body ached. Worst of all, though, my eyes burned and the base of my skull throbbed.

"Well, if it makes you feel any better, we've just completed the equivalent of five hours of trauma surgery." He smirked at me. "We just feel the pain differently than surgeons do. Their feet and lower backs hurt. Our heads hurt." I nodded.

"Did you ever watch *M*A*S*H?*" I asked him, moving only my eyes to look at him.

"Sure."

"I remember this one episode. Hawkeye sees a friend of his from high school. He later operates on the friend and loses him on the table. He is distraught." Jason nodded.

"So after surgery, Henry comes to talk to Hawkeye. Henry tells him that when he went to school for commanding officers, he learned that there are two rules of war. Rule number one is that young men die. Rule number two is that doctors can't change rule number one."

Jason looked away from me, staring at the wall ahead of him. We sat together in silence for a long minute. Finally, in an exaggerated motion, he sat up and helped me do the same.

That afternoon, feeling useless to do anything else, I wrote in my journal about the two rules. I found myself astonished that even fifty years after the Korean War, some things still seemed very much the same. We still heard the helicopters coming, waited for them, ducked our heads, and ran to bring our patients in on canvas stretchers. We still wrote on patients' chests with ink so their next doctors would know what we had done, and we still operated on gurneys made into OR tables.

There were differences too, of course. With body armor that often protected our warriors from fatal torso injuries, perhaps Henry's line to Hawkeye would be slightly different today. Rule number one might now state that war damages people. Rule number two, of course, would be unchanged.

I was certain of one truth, though, that Henry might not have learned in his course fifty years ago: War damages doctors, too. They are damaged by rule number two.

The House of God

The medical officer for Naval Mobile Construction Battalion, a Navy Captain, happened to be a psychiatrist. Jason knew him from his time with the Marines, and I knew him from my aviation tours. We both liked and respected him.

A short time after we conducted those marathon debriefing groups for his Seabees, Captain Koffman contacted me to say he would be visiting Al Asad to check on his battalion and asked to meet with Jason and me. He also invited Gary, the psychologist assigned to the Marine infantry battalion on base. Gary operated in isolation much of the time due to the frequency of his Marines' missions outside the wire (off the base). When I imagined how difficult it would be for me if I were in his place, I worried about him a little.

When the captain arrived, the three of us were waiting. He wore the uniform of the Seabees. We entered our small office space and closed the door, taking seats that faced each other.

"So," Captain Koffman began, making eye contact with each of us. "Since I was here anyway, I wanted to use this opportunity to check in with the three of you."

Having expected questions about the Seabees, we sat in surprised silence.

"You've been here over two months."

We nodded.

"How are you doing?" He spoke the words deliberately, dark eyes focused intently on us.

We glanced at one another, shifting in our chairs. I cleared my throat.

"Uh, well, I think we're fine, sir."

Clearly unconvinced, he moved his eyes to Jason and Gary, who nodded in earnest agreement.

"What sorts of things are you seeing most?"

We were ready for that one. We knew the number of patients our little clinic had seen, the diagnosis categories, and our medevac numbers, which were low.

"These Marines, they don't want to be sent home," we told him. He nodded.

"So we tend to keep them out here with us."

"Is it mostly Marines you are treating?" he asked. "What about the medical providers with you? Are you able to help them process some of what they are witnessing?"

Jason and I laughed. "They don't want anything to do with that, sir," Jason said. "There was one case we dealt with, a little girl. Pretty traumatic for everyone. After that, some of them asked to talk. But for the most part, everyone's doing okay. At least that's what they're telling us."

"Do you believe them?"

"I don't know. Everyone seems like they're hanging in there. It's been a long couple of months."

"How are you dealing with it all?" he asked.

Not unlike the way our reluctant patients often looked at us, we sat quietly and stared at him. Four shrinks in one small room, I mused in silence, hiding a tiny grin. Someday, I imagined, I would think back on this moment and chuckle.

"How are the Seabees doing now, sir?" Jason asked. The captain smiled a little and took the bait, thanking us for our care of the Al Asad battalion. Happy for Jason's skillful deflection of the senior psychiatrist's attention, I mentioned that Jason and I had attended the Seabees' memorial service, adding that I had not realized how much I missed our national anthem until it was played that day. I think I said something about that moment, the sudden appreciation of "The Star-Spangled Banner," being one I would never forget.

The captain asked about other moments we would remember. Jason and Gary paused, so I jumped in.

I told him about Dunham. I intended my story to be brief, focusing on the fascinating clinical details about the changing status of his head injury and the strength of his spirit. But somehow it ended up about us, about our connection with our Marine, about the delusional hope that he would recover, about the crushing news of the death we all knew in our hearts was inevitable.

I felt tears pool in my eyes and blinked at them angrily.

"Oh, for Pete's sake," I muttered, mortified. "I mean, how many times have I told this story? What is wrong with me?"

The captain smiled kindly at me, saying nothing.

Gary started speaking then, surprising all of us with a vivid description of a horrific scene at which he arrived as a first responder.

"— the Marine's face was gone," Gary ended, and swallowed hard. My own embarrassment forgotten, I leaned forward to touch Gary's sleeve.

"I wish you would have come over," I breathed, searching for eye contact. "Please, Gary, don't go through something like that alone again. We're right here . . ."

He looked up, eyes misty, and smiled slightly at me. I knew he wouldn't ask for my help, but he appreciated my offering it.

And so it began. We talked about casualties, about the strain of listening to the grief and fear and loss of our patients all day, about sometimes having no idea what to say, about the incoming rockets and the baking heat at night and the contractors beheaded on video. Most of all, we talked about fatigue. We were tired, we told him, and we'd only been out here two months.

Captain Koffman listened to us for almost two hours. When he left our office that day, offering to drop Gary off at the regiment, Jason and I sat for a moment in silence together before we looked at each other.

"Well. That was interesting," I started.

Jason nodded. "That was group therapy. That's what that was."

"You know," I commented, as we rose to gather our covers and sunglasses from the desk, "I'm wondering if Captain Koffman really came out here just to check on the Seabees."

"It's pretty clear he was here today for one reason," Jason said. "He was here to check on us."

Later that evening, writing in my journal about our cathartic group, I remembered a book I had had to read in school. *The House of God*, by Samuel Shem, an entertaining and heartbreaking story about medical interns, had almost nothing to do with our experience out here — except for one character's words, which popped into my mind now. He said, "How can we care for patients if nobody cares for us?"

We never forgot how the captain cared for us that day.

Mr. Oda

Special Forces (SF) soldiers are their own breed, and the ones who worked out of the secret compound hidden on our base were no exception. They wore civilian clothes and had longer hair; they appeared just slightly unshaven, and occasionally one would have a goatee. Their "concealed" pistols were obvious. Several of them loitered around the hospital, offering help if we needed it, since they were as skilled in first aid as any emergency medical technician. We soon figured out that these men were not spending their free time with us for altruistic reasons. The majority of the women on the base worked at the hospital.

"Excuse me?"

I looked up from the notes I was writing at the nurses' station.

"I'm Trent, from SF."

Trent was almost too good-looking, with a chiseled face, tanned skin, and intense brown eyes, one of which was hidden beneath long bangs. He smiled as he extended his hand. His teeth were straight and slightly too white.

"Hi." He grinned.

"Afternoon." I shook his hand without standing. "I'm Heidi Kraft."

"Nice to meet you, Heidi," he said. (A group of us later laughed at the fact that although he was a staff sergeant in the Army, Trent somehow managed to be just Trent, even to an officer in the Navy. And a lieutenant commander, clearly marked with an obvious gold maple leaf on her collar, became just Heidi. For some reason, he could get away with it.)

"What can I do for you?" I asked now, signing my discharge note illegibly and placing it in a stack.

"We have this problem . . . or rather . . . a situation . . . that's come up," he began. "I was hoping to ask you your opinion."

"Sure." I pointed to the chair next to me.

He looked around uneasily. "Is there a place we could talk" — he leaned forward and whispered — "privately?"

"No problem." I motioned for him to follow me next door to our psych ward.

Our ward, a tiny room with a padlocked door, contained whitewashed concrete walls, a single sandbagged window, and two cots. Three two-by-fours hanging by traction from cord strung across nails functioned as unsteady shelves. Trent sat on one cot and I sat on the other. I propped one of the flat pillows against the wall, leaned back, and raised one boot over my knee.

"Okay, what's up?"

"We have this Iraqi informant. He's very important to us and has already given us information that's led to the arrest of an insurgent leader. We have been keeping him safe since then. He has everything he needs, a bed, food, satellite TV . . . but none of us can really communicate with him, and now that the translators are busy with other things, it's been a while since anyone's really talked to him. Apparently he thinks he's a prisoner."

"Is he?" It was an innocent question.

"No. We're keeping him safe until we can get him out of the country . . . it's kind of the equivalent of the Iraqi witness protection program. There are several of us who've been working on getting him a new identity . . . but we've been really busy, and our chain of command needs to approve our plans. It's no excuse, but it wouldn't be safe for him to leave."

"Where does psych come in?"

Trent exhaled. He finally got to the important part. "He tried to kill himself last night."

"How?"

"He wrapped the cord from his lamp around his neck and tried to plug himself in. We came in just in time and several of us tackled him, but it would have totally fried him if we hadn't." I tried to imagine "plugging himself in," but it was hard to conceptualize. Trent seemed to realize that. "Basically, he *became* the lamp. Anyway, he's not talking to anyone now, just crying all the time and praying and saying he wants to leave. We're afraid he's going to try again."

"Sounds like he's pretty depressed." Having stated the obvious, I made the obvious suggestion. "Is there a possibility you guys can talk to him more, explain where you are in your plans to let him get on with his life? Make him feel like he's not a prisoner, since he's not."

"You think that would help?"

"I have no idea. I haven't met the patient."

"Do you want to?"

"Um. Well, no, not really. I mean, how would I interview him?"

"I could bring you some civilian clothes, some jeans maybe. We would take you to him, we could have tea and you could tell us what questions to ask and we could ask him. That way he wouldn't know you were interviewing him."

"What do you mean, he wouldn't know?"

"Well, you would be sitting away from the table, and you could be telling the interpreter what questions you want asked. Women do not sit at the same tables as men in Iraq."

"I see. Well, tell you what — how about you guys make sure this patient knows he's *not* actually a prisoner, and let's see if that works. I'm not sure what good I would do him in that sort of context. Okay?"

"Okay. Thanks, Doc." We stood up and he extended his hand.

"Sure thing. Good luck."

The next morning at rounds, all ten of our company's doctors sat hip to hip, crammed on two facing cots in the call room. We discussed the patients on the ward, and I had started to tell them about my interesting run-in with Trent when there was a knock at the door. He was standing there, brown hair in his eyes and huge arms obvious in his easy-fitting cotton shirt. He didn't flinch in front of ten Navy officers, just looked at me and said, "Can I talk to you, Doc?"

The news had gone from bad to worse. The nonprisoner/patient had attempted suicide again this morning, taking all ten sleeping pills he had been given by the unit doctor. The Special Forces guys wouldn't have known that, however, if he hadn't also taken the blades out of his razor and sliced up his arms and legs in a gory, but not lethal, attempt to bleed to death. The soldiers saw the blood on the floor when they came and checked on him, realized he was unconscious, and brought him to the hospital.

"He's here now?"

"Yep." So much for wearing jeans and having tea.

"Okay, bring him back."

The nurses checked the patient in, took vitals, and made up a chart for me. At the bottom of the page, since we didn't know his real name and the SF guys weren't about to tell us, they wrote *ODA*.

ODA. Other Defense Agency. The first time we saw one of them, an enemy prisoner of war, Karen thought that *Oda* was the guy's last name and referred to him for two days as Mr. Oda. The name stuck.

Walking down the passageway to the ward, I wondered what this Mr. Oda would think of being evaluated by an American military woman. Women did not drink tea with men in this country, let alone perform psychiatric evaluations

144

of them. I glanced at the pistol hanging from my shoulder holster. I was sure he would love me. I knocked and entered cautiously.

Mr. Oda sat on a cot, his head down and shoulders slumped. He was a small man with a bony frame and a small mustache. His off-white traditional *thoub* was splattered with blood.

"Hello," I said quietly. "I am Dr. Kraft." He looked up, met my eyes for a fleeting moment, and then turned to face the interpreter, who translated. I extended my hand, but he did not take it. I sat on the cot opposite him and leaned forward.

"The soldiers here are worried about you," I started. He kept his head lowered but raised his eyes to the interpreter. "They are worried that you want to end your life. Is that true?"

He talked to the interpreter then, gesturing wildly with his hands. His wide eyes appeared frenzied. The interpreter waited until he stopped and then summarized for me. "I am a prisoner! I just want my freedom. I want to leave. I tried to tell them, but they would not listen."

"Were you in fact trying to end your life? Do you want to die?"

"Yes."

"Why?"

He began to cry. His pressured speech was heavy with emotion, even through the language barrier. "I have nothing . . . to live for . . . no one . . . I don't deserve to be alive . . ."

I took a deep breath. I needed to get some history. This would be slower going than I had expected.

It took nearly an hour to learn that his family was from nearby. He was one of many children. His cousin was the insurgent whose demise was sealed when the patient provided information to the Americans. He had been engaged, but after the arrest of his cousin, his fiancée was "gone." He was twenty-four. He looked fifty.

We ended our conversation with a deal. I agreed to talk to the Special Forces CO and urge him to find a way to get the patient out of the country. He agreed not to kill himself on our ward. A very tall American soldier, with a 9mm in the pocket of his jean shorts, stayed with Mr. Oda, just in case.

I asked Trent to send for his commanding officer, then I left the building, covered in a fine dusting of grime, to watch *The Sopranos* with the guys. We had not finished the intro song to the episode when my radio barked. I ran down the back passageway to the hospital in time to see the lanky SF guy and Dave, our OR nurse, dragging the patient down the hall, his arms draped over their shoulders. "What happened?" I asked, moving toward them.

"We were smoking," explained Dave as he and the soldier lifted Mr. Oda and brought him through the door. The patient muttered loudly in Arabic, a trancelike cadence to his words. They helped him to the cot, where he lay down, buried his head in the pillow, and began to weep.

"When we looked away, he lifted the big cement ashtray and crushed it over his head."

"Please," I said, approaching Mr. Oda.

He sat up then, looked at me with wild eyes, and began bashing his head against the cement wall.

"Please, you need to stop doing that. I will try to help you . . ." I reached out and touched his sleeve. He cringed as if my fingers had burned his flesh and curled up on the cot, knees drawn to his chest. He continued to slam his head backward against the cement, repeating the same anguished words in Arabic again and again. I turned to the SF guy. "Do *not* let him keep doing that — is that clear?" He had been sitting, but he nodded and got to his feet.

I left the ward and radioed Jason, ran the situation by him in thirty seconds flat, and relayed his order for intramuscular Haldol, a quick-acting antipsychotic medication, to calm the man down. I could not understand Mr. Oda, so I had no idea if his ranting words were psychotic and dangerous or simply an expression of grief from a man who had made the gut-wrenching choice of betraying his family. HM2 Patacsil gave him the shot.

Mr. Oda's eyelids fluttered. He rested his head on the pillow and shut them. I breathed a sigh of relief.

"I don't have time to wait for your captain to come tomorrow," I told the tall soldier. "I'm going to need to have this patient leave this ward tonight. Can you relay that message?"

"Yes, ma'am."

One hour later the CO arrived with Trent and several others. I explained to him that Mr. Oda was suicidal but that I couldn't ascertain whether that was due to serious mental illness or not, since I couldn't understand him. "For surgeons, this doesn't matter," I said. "For us, it's everything. I'm sorry . . . we tried. But we can't take care of him here."

He tried to argue with me, but I was determined, so he left, saying he would "make a few phone calls." When Mr. Oda awoke, the captain and four other civilian-clad soldiers joined him in the ward, closed the door, and presented him with some options. When the door opened an hour later, Mr. Oda was laughing. I came to the doorway.

"Are you going to be okay?" the interpreter asked him for me.

"Yes," he said, smiling and standing. He briefly looked at me, and then talked to the interpreter, who translated. "He says for me to tell the lady doctor that he cannot thank you enough for being so kind to him. He says that you remind him of his mother." Mr. Oda came forward then, took my hand, and shook it, all the while keeping his head bowed. I lowered my own head in deference to what I now know to be the ultimate compliment from an Arab man.

The captain stepped forward to shake my hand as the other four escorted the patient down the hall.

"Hey, Captain, what's going to happen to him?"

"We're giving him a car and money and he's driving himself to a destination we determined."

"Not tonight, he's not," I objected. "He's still got Haldol on board."

"When can he drive? Tomorrow morning?"

I admitted that he could. The captain nodded. Mr. Oda giggled as he walked. He was feeling no pain. All four of them walked with him down the hallway. I watched them disappear out the back door of the hospital.

My watch said 2300. I leaned against the wall, totally exhausted as the adrenaline left my body. "Good-bye, Mr. Oda," I whispered to myself, ". . . and Godspeed."

One week later Trent lingered around the hospital again, talking to one of the female corpsmen. He saw me coming to the call room for rounds.

"Hey, Doc," he called out, leaving his chair by his friend and walking over. "Did you hear about your patient?"

"Well, he was never officially my patient . . ." I read his eyes for clues but found none. "But how is he?"

"Dead. We found him a few days ago. He was shot about twenty times. I guess he took a wrong turn."

"A wrong turn."

"Yeah."

Reality

"Just so we're clear, ma'am, I am *not* here because I need help. My Gunny told me I had to come, so here I am."

"I understand, Private. Please, have a seat."

I fought to focus my parched, stinging eyes on the young Marine as he sat down and rested his rifle across his thighs. The sandstorms of the past few weeks had included a howling, fierce summer wind that sucked the breath from our lungs in hot, painful surges. I have never walked into an actual blast furnace but imagine it would be a similar sensation. My eyes suffered as well.

The private sitting before me was sent to us by his command. The gunnery sergeant who accompanied the patient spoke of "erratic behavior" and "scaring people in his shop." He mentioned they had recently learned that the Marine had had a previous psychiatric hospitalization. Before I saw the patient, I asked our techs to contact the Naval medical center for details of his admission.

"How have things been going for you during this deployment?" I started my interview casually.

"Great. I love it here." The Marine grinned widely at me.

"Your Gunny is worried about you, Private. He believes you've been acting differently lately."

"Really." The Marine, who had been making infrequent eye contact and mostly looking out the window, suddenly turned light blue eyes on me.

When I met his gaze, he flashed a phony smile. I began a standard psychiatric interview, starting with basic questions of demographics and symptoms, which he answered curtly but appropriately. I asked if he had ever been seen by a mental health professional prior to today. The smile faded. He nodded yes but refused to provide details. I asked about a family history of psychiatric problems. He laughed then — a deep, throaty sound that caused the hairs on the back of my neck to stand up.

"My family is fucking nuts. Isn't everyone's?"

I smiled. This was a reasonable attempt at humor, although the laugh still made me uncomfortable.

"Have you ever been hospitalized on a psychiatric ward?"

"Sure."

"How long were you in the hospital?"

"I don't know. Three days?"

"What can you tell me about that?"

"Nothing."

"I can't help you without some history about what has happened."

"I told you. I don't want your help." His unbroken gaze penetrated the space between us. He was no longer smiling.

"Okay, fair enough. Let's talk about something else. What

can you tell me about shouting at your Ka-bar [the Marine Corps–issued knife] in the shop the other day?"

"She pissed me off. I later apologized."

"Your Ka-bar pissed you off?"

"Yeah. But these things happen." He began stroking the muzzle of the M16 on his lap. "She understood. Just like this one — she does, too. It's not a good thing, you know?"

"What's not a good thing?"

"The sun. If it's allowed to penetrate directly, it can actually derail a train."

"We were talking about your Ka-bar."

"Don't you think I know that?" he said angrily, the volume of his voice increasing. "Of course I do. It's all just a matter of timing." He jerked his head and stared at the far corner of the ceiling. I followed his gaze.

"Are you looking at something up there?"

He refocused on me. "No." He chuckled. "You think that's what this is about, don't you? It's not like I never sang in the church choir, okay?"

"Okay. Do you mind if we talk about your Ka-bar again? I am having a difficult time understanding what you are telling me."

"You are making fun of me." He narrowed his icy eyes.

"No, Private. I am absolutely not making fun of you. I am trying to understand, Private." I used his rank often in an attempt to defuse his obvious agitation, to remind him he was a U.S. Marine. It appeared to work. The boot he had been tapping on the deck stopped for a moment.

Just then, Petty Officer Patacsil knocked. I asked the patient to excuse me and closed the door as I exited the room.

"Ma'am," Patacsil said in hushed tones. "I talked to the hospital. He was admitted last year, right after he got to his first unit. He remained on the psych ward for — get this — two weeks. His working diagnosis was schizophrenia, but the records show he was returned to duty."

Schizophrenia is a psychiatric diagnosis that refers to psychotic symptoms such as hallucinations, delusions, and other disorganized thinking.

"How strange," I mused. "He must have made a full recovery without meds, and they must have changed their minds about their original diagnosis. Maybe it was due to a head injury or drugs. Any mention of other collateral information?"

"No, ma'am."

"Okay, thanks. Hey, hang around out here, all right?" He nodded. I was thankful to know he was right outside.

I re-entered the room. The patient was tapping his foot again and grinding his teeth so loudly I could hear them.

"What was that about?" he snapped. "I know what you're trying to do. You want to fillet me, like a fucking hamster."

"My corpsman called the hospital to find out about your stay there, Private. They said you were there fourteen days, not three."

As quickly as it had arrived, the look of agitation left his face, replaced by unnerving calm. He smiled without showing teeth.

"Does your husband ever forget your birthday?"

"I beg your pardon?"

"People forget things. It's anything but an admission of guilt; I just want you to know that."

"Private," I began softly. "I have to be honest with you. I am concerned that you are having some difficulties out here that require medical attention."

He squinted maliciously at me. The volume of his voice rose with each word until he was shouting. "What are you talking about? I never asked for this. My Ka-bar is fine. And you — you only wanted to fillet me anyway. None of this makes sense. I want to leave *now*."

"I would like you to come into the hospital," I stated firmly. "We can make sure that you are safe there."

He stared at me, unblinking.

"Private, please, let me help you."

In one fluid motion, my patient swung his M16 around on his lap so that it pointed almost, but not quite, directly at me. In an instant, I noticed that the magazine was inserted and his finger was resting above the trigger.

"I want to leave *now*," he repeated, teeth clenched.

"Sure. Sure, go right ahead."

The rifle remained pointed in my direction as he stood up and moved away. He opened the door, swung the weapon over his shoulder, and nonchalantly walked out past Petty Officer Patacsil, who was hovering there.

I sat motionless in my chair for a moment, stunned by

what had just transpired. As I replayed the session in my head, I remembered my Management of Violent Patients course during internship, where we learned how to subdue and restrain psychiatric patients, if needed. *There was never any mention of what to do if a patient aims a loaded rifle at you,* I thought.

I walked into the passageway, amazed that I could force my weak knees to move. I asked the Gunny to brief his CO that the Marine needed to be restrained and brought to the hospital. I asked Patacsil to tell the medevac team that I would be sending a psychotic patient out of country as soon as they could get a helicopter.

The four hours it took for the private's unit to deliver him to the hospital felt like weeks. He arrived unarmed and subdued, and walked quietly to the ward. Jason assumed his care at that time, to avoid the possibility of agitating the patient with my presence.

I happened to be in the ward as the medevac arrived and the patient was escorted out to the waiting helicopter. I sat in the nurses' station and waited.

The roar of the rotor blades increased as the helicopter lifted off. The private would return home, where a team at the naval hospital was waiting for him. He would be treated and then medically retired from the Marine Corps, with Veterans Administration disability for a psychotic break on active duty.

I sat down for a moment and closed my eyes. They stung mercilessly. The night before, we had crossed out day 112 on Jason's wall calendar with a bold red *X*. According to our conservative estimate, we were exactly halfway through the deployment.

The fatigue, or that blast furnace of a summer wind, was starting to take its toll.

The Best We Could

Early one morning in the week before Memorial Day, a brown Humvee skidded around the corner near the hospital and screeched to a halt in front of the building. The driver leaped out and sprinted inside, tripping and falling with a crash at the front desk. His anguished, screamed words echoed through the passageways of the facility.

"Someone help me!"

Within seconds, five of our corpsmen stood at the rear entrance to his vehicle and carefully lifted a young Marine onto a gurney. The patient's desert uniform was soaked with blood. Our litter bearers moved through the front door, one of them starting CPR as they progressed down the hall to the SST. A crimson trail dripped behind them, marking their path.

Several minutes later, three men and one woman emerged from the Humvee, moving as if in a trance toward the hospital. The woman's hands were completely red. She stopped in the front lobby, saw the blood on the deck, and raised her hands to her face. She paused a moment and then ran her fingers through her light brown hair.

All four were covered with blood. Surgical company corpsmen ushered them toward the sick call area. Despite the dramatic stains on their uniforms, none of them was injured. My combat stress team was called soon after.

When Petty Officer Gob and I arrived, the corpsmen at the front desk of the surgical company filled us in on what had transpired. We moved into the triage area and found the three men and one woman sitting together on a cot in the passageway, all of them staring vacantly at the deck. We introduced ourselves and escorted them to the small waiting area near the OR, providing cold bottles of water and rolls of toilet tissue.

They drank. A few poured water onto their hands and splashed it on their faces. The woman, whose cheeks and eyes were streaked with bloody fingerprints and whose hair was matted in wet red clumps, made no move to rinse off. She gazed at her boots with unblinking eyes. Her collar insignia identified her as her unit's corpsman.

Our company commander touched me lightly on the shoulder then, whispering that the Marine in the SST had passed away. She said that the surgeons were still with other patients. Could I handle telling the group? Stunned, I said nothing. She took that as a yes.

I peered in the doorway at the foursome. One of them was a junior officer, a chaplain. We made eye contact, and I asked him if we could speak outside.

"Chaplain, I'm sorry to tell you, but the Marine you brought in today has died."

He gasped slightly, biting his lip. His eyes immediately filled with tears. "Oh no," he said. "No. Not this boy."

"I am very sorry for your loss," I whispered. He nodded.

"We are a reserve unit," he explained, tears streaking his dirty cheeks. "Some of our members have been together almost twenty years, including — including this boy's uncle, who is out here too."

My eyes widened. "What a loss for your unit. It sounds like you're very close."

He nodded.

"Chaplain, would you like to tell your colleagues the news of your Marine's death, or would you like me to do it?"

He straightened his shoulders. "I'll do it. It should come from me."

Gob and I entered the room with him. The two Marines and the corpsman looked up. The chaplain started to talk, but his words became tangled in the sob that burst from his throat. "You tell them," he whispered, and he crumpled into a chair, lowering his face to his hands.

I faltered, realizing I did not even know the Marine's name. I started speaking empty words, stating that although we had tried very hard to revive their colleague, his injuries were too serious . . .

I did not finish my sentence. There was no need.

They began to cry. The three men rose from their chairs, moved to the corpsman, and kneeled on the hard tile beside her. They wrapped their arms around her tightly as she wailed in despair. Gob and I slowly backed out of the room.

I walked to the lobby to make arrangements with our front-desk clerk to meet the reserve unit's CO when he arrived. As I started to return to the waiting room, a movement caught my eye.

Petty Officer Tomat, a corpsman from our company, jumped down from the back of the Humvee still parked in front of the hospital. I watched as she carefully lifted a large bucket from the vehicle's open hatch and proceeded to dump it out in the sand. The water was dark red. She walked to the entrance of the hospital and began to fill the empty bucket with sponges and towels, preparing to put them away. I approached her.

"Petty Officer Tomat, did someone ask you to clean this vehicle?"

"No, ma'am."

"Why did you do it?"

She shrugged. "I just didn't want those guys who lost their friend to have to do it."

She picked up the bucket and stripped off her gloves.

"They're all our Marines, ma'am. It's just what we do."

I returned to the OR waiting room. The four of them still sat together, weeping softly. Gob hovered in the passageway. His eyes told me he was standing by but that his services had not been requested.

As the two of us moved away from the door, pulling it closed to allow them some privacy, the four people inside moved together, arms wrapped around one another, to form a tight circle. All four heads leaned in to touch in the center. As the door clicked shut, we heard one of the men repeating the same words over and over.

Although I knew he spoke specifically about their situation, I found myself strangely comforted by his words. After all, they applied to us, too.

"We did the best we could."

HOME

I met Margy and Colette in flight surgeon school, and they became my best friends in the Navy. All three of us fell in love with Marine officers. This was a source of constant entertainment for the men in our lives.

Margy's husband, Hunter, a Hornet pilot, had deployed with a Marine ground combat unit as an air officer during the initial invasion of Iraq in early 2003. (Marine Corps aviators regularly serve with ground units to coordinate air and ground combat operations.) After several long, dark months of no communication with him and constant worry, we were tremendously relieved when he came home.

The night before I left for Iraq, Hunter gave me his leather pistol holster, along with words of advice and concern that could only have come from someone who had been there. And one day in early June, he wrote to me.

From what I've heard, things have heated up again. I'm sure you understand now what I was trying to tell you before you left. The hardest thing is to retain your composure when Marines get killed or badly injured. I know how you feel.

It was the most challenging thing to me to force myself to keep it together when I felt like I was going to lose it and say, "Is this worth it?"

Just know that it is. The junior Marines and Sailors around you are looking to you for strength and positive guidance. Our colonel was great at keeping everything in perspective. I hope there is someone of that caliber there with you to help guide you in the right direction.

I can't tell you how appreciative Margy and I are of what you are doing. We talk about you every day and pray (I don't do that very much) for your speedy and safe return. I wish you were not there, but at the same time, I'm very glad that you are. The Marines need someone like you there. You are their "mom" for lack of a better term. I know it has a very positive impact.

Margy and I just got back from our Memorial Day retreat to (of all places) Joshua Tree. I hadn't been camping in the desert enough, so off we went. It was like old times, except no one was shooting at me.

Keep your head down and your Kevlar on. XOXO, Hunter.

Hero,
Part II

One day in mid-June, I found some time to get to the Internet café and check my e-mail. The *from* line of one of my messages caused me to freeze at the keyboard.

It said *Deb Dunham (Jason's Mom)*.

I paused for a long minute before opening the e-mail. It was written to both Karen and me, and started *Dear Ladies, my name is Deb Dunham. Corporal Jason L. Dunham is my son.*

I drew in a sharp breath and felt the tension in my fingers as they gripped the mouse. I was aware of a sensation of two large hands gripping my intestines and squeezing. I read on.

> I received a copy of the letters that you sent to Mike Phillips. As Jason's mom, I need to thank both of you remarkable women. The reason I am writing one letter to both of you is — I don't think I can write this more than once.

She continued, describing her worry about Jason's deployment and the discussion she and her husband had had with their son when he was home at Christmas regarding his wishes should he be injured in Iraq. She shared the details of the night they received the call with the news that Jason was in critical condition. She told me that she started out praying he would be all right, but then suddenly, in the middle of the night, changed her prayer to ask God that her son not be alone or afraid.

> To the both of you, I will never be able to thank you enough for taking such good care of my son. I could not hold his hand, talk to him or help him in any way. I thank you for doing what I wanted to do for my son as his mother, but was not able to do.

She described seeing her son at Bethesda. She told me that they considered it a great gift to be present to witness the "peace on his face once the pain left his body."

Tears flooded my eyes and blurred the letters. I closed my eyes tightly for a moment and then refocused on her final words.

> Some reporter asked my husband if we were not proud of our son for dying a hero . . . Heidi and Karen, you are definitely my heroes and I will be thanking God every day for the rest of my life for the part you played in taking care of my son.
>
> Much love to you, Deb Dunham.

I clasped my hands together in my lap. They were trembling violently. My chest shuddered with every breath. My attempts to keep my tears unnoticed by the Marines sitting around me were useless. Several of them stared. I sat frozen for a long minute and sobbed silently. From that moment forward, I knew — as I closed the e-mail, gathered my things, and left the room to find Karen — I would never be the same again.

HOME

I wrote an e-mail to my group of family and friends in late June to share the wonderful news. In the middle of my clinic that morning, my radio had crackled: "Oscar Four Kilo, this is Oscar Four Bravo."

"Go ahead," I said.

"Just wanted to tell you that Rhys has arrived." The elation in Jason's voice was obvious, even over the radio. I squealed in delight and told him I'd be right there. I ran the whole way.

He had been calling his wife after breakfast every possible day for the past month, I wrote to my e-mail group. This morning she did not answer the home phone, so he called her cell. She was at the hospital, in labor. He stayed on the phone the entire time, even hearing the baby's first cry.

In my e-mail home, I described our baby shower celebration. Bill, Steve, and I ordered an outfit from Baby Gap, and we hung IT'S A BOY streamers around their barracks room. Blue balloons, paper plates, and Hostess cupcakes with candles stuck in them created a small but happy party in honor of Jason's new son.

Jason smiled at us with genuine thanks. But I saw the pain in his eyes. My babies were not babies anymore; they were twenty-one months old, but I felt it nonetheless. And I understood.

A baby shower in Iraq. Once again, I wrote that day, two concepts — like combat and mental health — that seemed mutually exclusive.

The Optimists

Our Independence Day was celebrated in Iraq with a small barbecue and no fireworks. Since then, the scorching days dragged on, bad copies of one another, with each morning's intelligence report including the same weather forecast: "Hot, windy, and a high of one hundred thirty-two." Despite my best attempts to stay in the shade, the thick sleeves of my uniform occasionally did come between my arms and the sun. I remained as motionless as possible at those times, hoping the cotton would not touch my skin. I could almost hear the sizzle if it did.

The power had been out on the base for nearly six weeks. With no working fans to stop the sand flies, their bites peppered our legs, itching mercilessly and swelling into tiny welts. At night our concrete barracks, which withstood incoming mortars with impressive strength, became brick ovens with more than one-hundred-degree temperatures and no moving air. Our sleep was interrupted when the water we sprayed on our arms and legs had evaporated, along with its temporary relief. At that point, we awakened to respray and flip over, like rotisserie chickens. Deep shadows circled our eyes. We rested our chins in our palms between bites of breakfast.

My eleven o'clock patient on this particular day was a no-show. I wandered out of the office and bought a cold Coca-Cola Light from the Iraqi vendor in the theater, who had ice in large coolers. I held it to my cheek before cracking it open. Sometimes, *heaven* was redefined.

There was a knock on our office door, which was ajar. The Marine standing there glanced around uneasily before entering.

"Good morning, ma'am." His baritone voice was raspy. "I'm looking for Dr. Kraft."

"That's me." I stood and extended my hand.

"Master Sergeant Boone." He grasped my hand firmly. "Do you have a minute, ma'am?"

The master sergeant wore a dirty desert-tan flight suit with a pistol strapped to his thigh and attached to the green web belt that hung loosely from his waist. His gray hair was shaved so short he was nearly bald. His brown, leathery skin was etched with deep grooves. I considered offering him one of the samples of sunscreen I had in my pocket but decided against it, quite sure of his answer. Oil and dirt were caked onto his hands, and grime stuck under the remnants of his fingernails, which were chewed to the quick. He raised a fist to cover a cough.

"Doc Green sent me," he began, and coughed again. I took a sip of my Coke Light.

"He said you might be able to do hypnosis to help me stop smoking."

I nearly spit out the entire sip. "I beg your pardon. Did you say stop smoking?"

"Yes, ma'am."

I cleared my throat and covered my mouth to hide a smile. "Well, I do use hypnosis to assist with smoking cessation in the States — um — okay, how long have you been smoking, Master Sergeant?"

"Thirty-one years. I started when I was twelve."

"I see. And how much do you smoke?"

"I've just cut down to two packs a day." He seemed genuinely proud of himself.

"And you are absolutely sure that you want to try to quit out here, in Iraq?"

"I don't want to try, ma'am. I want to do it."

I smiled. He would succeed.

The master sergeant was on flight status, so he could not be prescribed Zyban, an antidepressant medication that helps some people with nicotine cravings. Otherwise, he embraced the entire behavioral program I established for him, including the monitoring of his smoking, identification of associated factors in his life, and daily practice of self-hypnosis techniques I taught him. I suggested to him under a trance state that Gatorade, his drink of choice with a cigarette, would lose its flavor while he was smoking. Two weeks later he arrived with a huge grin on his face. His teeth were badly stained, but his smile was contagious.

"I'm down to three cigarettes a day!" He beamed at me, sitting down.

"Congratulations! That is wonderful news. Have you noticed any other changes?"

"Well, now that you mention it —" He looked at me sideways and grinned. "Did you say something to me when I was under last time about Gatorade?"

"Why do you ask?"

"Well, it doesn't taste good anymore. At first I was bummed, because sitting on the porch of the squadron with the boys after a long day of flying, having a Gatorade and a smoke, was one of the only things I enjoyed about this place. Then it suddenly got this bizarre taste. So I figured, maybe you'd been messing with me, so I'd try it without a smoke. And what do you know — it tastes fine. Is that you doing that, Doc?"

"No, Master Sergeant. That's you doing that."

Word traveled fast in the staff noncommissioned officer network on our base. Within three weeks, five other senior enlisted Marines approached me for help with smoking cessation after they'd heard the master sergeant's success story. Five out of my group of six motivated smokers became smoke-free during our deployment. Only one Marine left treatment, explaining that after trying, he was more convinced than ever that people need to *start* smoking in Iraq, not stop.

The other five became very vocal about their victories. One saw me in line at the chow hall one day and loudly introduced me to his buddy. As we were parting, he called after me: "Hey, Doc — what do you call a Marine in a combat zone who smokes two packs a day and is worried about getting lung cancer someday?"

"I don't know. What do you call him?" I asked.

"An optimist."

HOME

During my sister's midsummer visit to my family in Florida, she took out the video camera and filmed the babies for me. A few weeks later, she edited that footage, burned it to a DVD, and sent it to me in a care package.

I waited several days before watching the DVD, in part because of an unusually busy clinic schedule and the fact that we had two patients on our ward. The other part I blame on my own hesitation to face the reality of what was taking place half a world away: my babies were becoming toddlers before everyone's eyes but mine.

One day after clinic, Karen joined me on our walk back to the barracks, and I asked if she wanted to watch the DVD with me. She enthusiastically agreed. We sat down together on my cot.

My children looked so happy.

They responded to their daddy, their grandparents, and their aunt Steph with that wonderful expression of joy that can only be found on the face of a twenty-one-month-old. Every little detail in their lives was extraordinary. I sat, mesmerized, staring at a little blond boy and a still-nearly-bald-but-becoming-blond girl, both of whom I almost did not recognize.

At one point in the film, Meg pulled herself up onto the sofa and sat there proudly, grinning for the camera. Brian followed her. When I left, nearly six months ago, they were nowhere close to accomplishing such a feat.

Everyone waved bye-bye to the camera on cue. Steph loudly proclaimed from behind the lens, "We love you, Mommy!" and the children joined in a cacophony of happy squeals. The screen of the DVD player went to static.

Karen looked at me with wide eyes. I pressed the stop button, avoiding her gaze.

"I don't know how it is that you are not crying right now," she exclaimed, wiping her eyes. "They're not even my babies, and I'm crying."

I looked at her and managed a small, closed-lipped smile as I placed the DVD back in its case.

"I decided five months ago that I couldn't let myself cry about them," I told her. "What good would it do to start now?"

Godspeed, Marines

Even an insurgent must draw the line somewhere. The last three weeks of July, we experienced consistent temperatures in the low 130s — and not a single rocket attack. We decided this was no coincidence. Despite the fact that the people actually doing the shooting were acclimated to the desert heat, we figured there must be a point at which even they decided it was just too hot. Regardless of the reason, we felt thankful for the reprieve; it was wonderful to become *accustomed*, again, to sleeping in silence.

We now carried our flak jackets and Kevlar helmets to work, stacking them in heavy piles in corners of the hospital. And we hiked the three quarters of a mile to chow without them, thirty pounds lighter. It was cause for celebration.

We should have known it was too good to last.

One of the last days in July, I was in a therapy session talking with a young lance corporal who suffered from recurrent nightmares. He had just begun a progressive muscle relaxation exercise by focusing on the muscles in his forehead when we heard a familiar, distant boom. He opened his eyes and we both looked out the window. In the next second, four explosions followed in rapid succession, each one louder — and closer to the hospital — than the one before it. The Marine and I got to our feet.

We retrieved our flak jackets and helmets quickly and moved away from the windows. We slid down the wall and sat on the tile as the windows rattled and the ground trembled beneath us. After a few minutes, the explosions ceased. We waited in the silence. It was over.

"Well," I said cheerfully, taking my patient's extended hand as he helped me up. "That was interesting."

The Marine grinned at me. "I better get back to my unit, ma'am. They'll be accounting for everyone." I nodded. We rescheduled his session.

After an attack, each unit conducted roll call to ascertain the whereabouts of all personnel. I penned a quick progress note for the session with the lance corporal, smiling ironically to myself as I wrote the words *session terminated due to incoming rockets.*

Nearly an hour later, wing headquarters sounded the all-clear, and everyone returned to work. Soon after, a walk-in patient arrived at our door.

He was a Seabee. I recognized his tanned face and graying crew cut; he was one of the Sailors who had attended our groups several months before. I introduced myself, aware of the tremor in his hand as he shook mine. I asked what I could do to help.

"Well, ma'am, I have been away from Al Asad since our unit met with you," he began. "I've been at a remote base, helping the Marines there with some projects. I just returned two weeks ago.

"I thought getting back to the battalion here would be good for me. I thought these things I've been dealing with would take care of themselves. And so far, I've been doing okay, until just about two hours ago."

"The rockets."

"Yes, ma'am." He sighed. "I guess I didn't realize how much they would bring back everything we did up there, everything we saw, everything . . ." His voice trailed off and he lowered his head.

"What can you tell me about being up there?" I asked quietly.

He looked up. "There was just a small group of us there, and a small group of Marines. We got really close to them. I think we told you our average age is thirty-eight? Well, their average age was not a day over nineteen." He smiled. "I think they looked at us almost like dads. It felt *so* great to be needed like that." He shook his head and pinched at the corners of his eyes, inhaling deeply.

"About three weeks ago, we had gone on a convoy to support some combat construction. When we returned, we got within about a half mile of our base, and the convoy stopped. I could see a plume of black smoke ahead, and several vehicles had obviously been hit by an IED. Lots of Marines were standing around them, looking up. They were watching a Phrog* as

---

*Nickname for CH-46, a Marine Corps transport helicopter.

it came in to land. Our convoy had been stopped so it could set down. Once the helo was on the ground, six Marines walked over together, stopping and looking down at a spot on the ground that I couldn't see. While we watched, they bent over and picked up a Marine's body. One of them took his head, two the arms, one the midsection, and two the legs. He was totally limp, like a rag doll. They pivoted around, walked to the bird, and loaded him in. Then they turned around and went back, leaning over to get another one. While we sat there, those Marines picked up the bodies of *four* men."

Tears welled in his brown eyes. He chewed on the inside of his cheek.

"It wasn't gruesome or anything, ma'am. That's it, what I just told you. But now, now that I'm back, I can't get that image out of my head. I see it whenever I'm alone; whenever it's quiet. It comes and I can't make it go away. I keep seeing it over and over and *over*. I keep seeing them putting those Marines' bodies in that helo." He blinked and allowed the waiting tears to run down his face.

"This was a tremendous loss for you," I stated simply. I swallowed, expecting a familiar lump in my throat. I found none.

The chief nodded.

"They were my friends, my little brothers, my — my sons," he whispered.

"How old is your own son, Chief Fitch?" I asked.

"My son?" He raised his eyebrows. I nodded.

"Almost seventeen, ma'am. He wants to enlist in the Marine Corps."

"Have you told him about this experience?"

He shook his head. "I wanted to protect him from stories like this."

We spent the rest of the hour talking about his family. As he left, I asked him to consider writing a letter to his son, describing his grief over the deaths of these young men. He said he would.

Chief Fitch returned in one week.

"The image has stopped, Doc," he said. "I don't see it anymore."

"Well, that is certainly good news. I know it was painful for you to keep seeing it. Can you attribute this change to anything?"

"Two things. First, I wrote that letter you suggested. I told my son that now I knew I was actually afraid of losing *him*. I told him he was everything to me, and that he had my support, whatever he wanted to do. I said if he wanted to become a U.S. Marine, nothing in the world would make me prouder."

I smiled.

"Second, I said good-bye to those Marines."

"Really? How?"

"Well, I couldn't sleep a couple nights ago. So I walked outside, lit a cigarette, and just sat there and looked at the stars. I waited for the image to come, which it did. I watched that Phrog land, and watched those Marines pick up those bodies. As much as I hated it, I forced myself to watch the whole thing without trying to stop it. And for the first time, I let the image keep going. I sat there and watched the helo actually lift off, tip its nose forward like they do, and fly away. I watched it fade away into the stars until I couldn't see it anymore.

"And I said out loud, 'Godspeed, Marines. It's time for me to let you go.' "

HOME

Late in July, I received an e-mail from Mike that caused my stomach to flip over. He told me that one of my colleagues at the hospital had called to say I was being extended for three additional months in Iraq, until December. I tracked down the message, which had originated from the Marines and asked for the extension of the deployment of medical augmentation personnel.

I found Cat and handed her the message. She began making phone calls.

As the day dragged on, I felt physical pain just thinking about having to stay longer. Tears welled in my eyes with no warning. Sometimes I thought of Mike and my babies and how much I wanted to see them in September. Sometimes I imagined the intense loneliness I would feel watching the people of this surgical company — who were all I had out here — go home without me. A sinking, heavy sensation of depression followed me throughout the day. I could not shake it.

At 2100, the guys and I sat in their barracks room watching

The Sopranos. I figured I might as well be distracted. Cat knocked on the door.

"You're coming home with us, ma'am."

It had been a mistake, a technicality. The message was sent by the Marines to all units who supported them, a blanket request for extension. Everyone else in my company had received the same message; the medical mobilization officers at Jacksonville simply did not understand it. They had told my department that I was staying without making sure they were correct.

I was furious. I was relieved. Most of all, I was thankful. I collapsed on my cot that night with prayers of thanksgiving. Several times throughout restless dreams, I bolted straight up, gasping for breath, my heart pounding.

Once again, the war invaded my sleep. But the feeling was different that night. Through those nightmares, I realized what I feared most.

It was being out here, alone, while my friends — who were now my family — went home without me.

One Hawkeye

After sunset, the entire base sank into deep shadows, but the Marine Air Wing compound didn't have the benefit of the inconsistent and wobbly street lights found around other areas. I depended on my squeeze flashlight as I walked around the headquarters building that night. I had met a pilot named Paul earlier that day, at the Internet café. He had noticed my flight psychologist wings, and after we'd been talking for a while about flying and people we both knew, he invited me to movie night. A group of the aviators who worked at the wing were planning to watch a DVD after their shift. I looked forward to the change of pace.

Following his directions, I walked along the makeshift wall that formed a perimeter around the wing barracks. Out of the darkness and silence I heard a voice. I jumped. Ten feet above the ground, in a watchtower, a Marine sentry talked on the radio. I murmured a silent prayer that he wouldn't see me and ask what the hell I was doing in the dark by myself. I had no idea what my answer would be.

Paul met me at the end of the perimeter wall, and I followed him to their barracks. The room he shared with an-

other aviator was tiny, but unlike our living arrangements —
in which nearly fifty women shared nine heads and six
shower stalls — they had their own bathroom. His mini–DVD
player was already set up with small computer speakers
attached, and a pile of movies had accumulated on the dusty
tile floor.

I sat on one of two cots in the room and leaned back against
the wall. Paul rummaged through a footlocker and retrieved
a plastic Listerine bottle that now held a clear liquid. He
poured it into a plastic squadron coffee mug and added a
packet of powdered Gatorade and some bottled water. He
stirred it with a plastic knife, handed it to me, unfolded a canvas stadium chair, and sat down facing me.

It tasted absolutely horrible, but I had to admit the numb-
ing effect of the vodka on my throat was comforting. For me,
because the helos could arrive at any time, a sense of dread
surrounded the idea of drinking alcohol. I was off duty tonight. I hadn't tasted a drop in more than five months. I figured I deserved it.

We talked as we passed the mug back and forth. He was a
helicopter pilot. This was his fourth deployment, second to
combat, and he was weary from his nonflying, twelve-hour
days monitoring message traffic. He asked about the things
that went on at the surgical company. He had no idea what
was happening two blocks away from him on the base. Like
all good aviators, he avoided the hospital like the plague. Once
I started telling him about my experience, I couldn't stop.

I told him about the sergeant with the eye injury, and about the triple amputee. I told him about Dunham. Paul did not say a word but breathed a heavy sigh.

I debated whether to continue. Today had been the worst. I looked at my boots, kicking my feet together.

"I was on duty today," I started quietly. Paul leaned forward, resting his elbows on his knees. "I was there at the hospital when a Humvee drove up in back. One of the independent-duty corpsmen from Division got out. He looked awful. We know him pretty well. He's brought us a lot of patients. I've been kind of worried about him with all the casualties their unit's taken.

"I said, 'Hey, Chief . . . how's it going?' He just stared at me. When he did talk, he sounded like a zombie, almost like he was slurring. He said, 'We couldn't find his . . . head . . . ' I focused beyond him and saw two of his guys walking up to the hospital with these large plastic bags. They were bringing them in as the chief was explaining the event to me.

"Apparently the bad guys are setting IEDs now in assembly-line fashion. One guy digs holes along the road, the next guy places the explosives in the holes, and the third fills the holes back in. Today, three combat engineers got out of their vehicles at one of these holes and were planning to fill the holes in before the explosives were placed, to interfere with the process. But apparently, the bad guys put the explosives in the mound of dirt next to the hole. One of the three Marines was bisected laterally, split in half the long way. Another lost both legs and his head. That's the one the chief was talking about. A third lost his entire abdominal cavity. There was nothing for medical to do. While I was talking to the chief, another vehicle pulled up. They had found the one Marine's head."

Paul swallowed hard. I felt certain I had broken every rule in the book, saying too much to a nonmedical person, especially one I barely knew. I searched his eyes and didn't see the answer. I went on.

"This was a long day, taking care of everyone involved. By about 1700 I felt totally deflated. I went to talk to Jason — he's my partner out here. And he's amazing. He's always, always here for me. So I started to tell him about the Marines and the plastic bags. But today he cut me off before I could finish. He said, 'Heidi, what can you and I do about this? Nothing. There is absolutely nothing we can do . . . so I just can't hear about it today.'

"I didn't know what to do . . . he is all I have out here. I mean, he's right, there's nothing we can do — and it's so hard on him, hearing about this from our patients all day — but —" I choked on the words, remembering how I fought at the time to hold back tears in front of Jason. I clenched my hands together in my lap and lowered my head as if in prayer.

"I was going to say . . ." Paul said quietly. "Everyone talks to you. Who do you talk to?"

I smiled wryly and looked up at him. "Who's the shrink for the shrink in a combat zone, right?" I shook my head.

The plastic squadron coffee mug was empty. Paul smiled warmly at me. It was one of those genuine smiles that told me he had no idea what to say but would sit there with me anyway. I closed my eyes for a moment. They stung.

We sat in silence for a short time. Then, obviously trying to change the subject, he cheerfully suggested that we look through his movies. He had a large selection, but we agreed that none really sounded good to watch that night. I took my leave.

The Marine sentry was still keeping watch in the tower. I waved at him. He waved back.

The shrink for the shrink in a combat zone, I realized, was simply that person who understood at any given moment. In the vast majority of those moments, that person for me was Jason. And most of the time, I trust that I was that person for him.

But if I had learned anything out here, it was that everyone needs a break sometimes.

So my shrink has also been a Navy nurse ten years my junior; the battalion chaplain who isn't even my religious denomination; and on this day, a helicopter pilot with no medical background whatsoever.

Drifting into unconsciousness that night, I thought of one of my favorite *M*A*S*H* episodes, the one in which Margaret and Hawkeye get caught under direct fire while helping out a small front-line unit. As the roof of the building collapses on them, Margaret looks at Hawkeye, frozen for an instant amid the roar of surrounding explosions. In that moment, she feels unconditional empathy from a person who, because of that moment in time, will be her friend forever.

I hope everyone who has ever served in any war has met at least one Hawkeye.

Woman's Best Friend

Sometimes, when a Black Hawk with its bright red cross landed on our pad in a swirl of dust, the patient brought in on the gurney was not a Marine, Sailor, Soldier — or even an enemy prisoner of war.

Sometimes the patient was a dog.

The Marines had a large corps of working dogs — beautiful, sinewy shepherds — who aided the mission in Iraq through the detection of explosives, weapons, and bad guys. Each dog had a Marine handler, and hundreds of these duos were spread throughout the country. The good news was the dogs were treated like royalty, with guaranteed air-conditioned spaces and terrific food. The bad news was sometimes they needed a doctor.

Our veterinarian was Army Major Tim Loonan, an extroverted man with a warm, engaging grin who had once been a paratrooper. Sharing resources with our operating room and intensive care unit had allowed Tim to build a complete animal surgical suite in the basement of the hospital. He knew of my fondness for dogs, so he sent word to me whenever he had a "lover" — a working dog that adored being adored. Not all of them fit this category. Whenever a lover arrived at Tim's shop, I found a way to spend some time in the basement, talking to the gorgeous animal while I stroked his head and kissed the bridge of his long nose. In Iraq, I developed a new appreciation for pet therapy.

I believe Tim knew how happy I was to have this unique opportunity to escape the desert for a few magical moments with his canine charges, but I do not believe I ever told him how much I appreciated his role in saving one of my patient's lives.

Sergeant Hutchinson, a petite brunette with freckles sprinkled across her nose, was a helicopter flight equipment specialist. Like many Marine pilots and aircraft maintenance personnel, she found herself in Iraq filling an unfamiliar role — in her case, as a member of an auxiliary support battalion. Grueling convoy duty took its toll on everyone in her company. But Sergeant Hutchinson had two other problems in addition to fatigue and vulnerability. She had a history of clinical depression, and she was the only woman in her company. She came to me early in the deployment feeling lethargic, weepy, hopeless, and fleetingly suicidal.

The sergeant and I had a heart-to-heart. She did not want to be sent home. Through tears, she begged to stay. Although she worried about how she would succeed, she said she wanted to finish the deployment to prove to both her unit and herself that she could. I believed her.

Jason and I worked together, combining antidepressant

medication and intensive therapy to teach her to block her self-defeating thought processes. For a while she made progress and slowly experienced more energy and increased self-worth.

Halfway through the summer, the sergeant experienced the loss of one of her friends in an IED explosion. This caused a downward spiral in her functioning that I feared pointed to her medevac. She told me her future was hopeless. She spoke of falling asleep and never awakening. She and I worked long into the evening that day, and I could almost hear her fingernails digging in as she struggled to maintain her grip on her mental health. She held on.

The operational tempo of her unit increased, and she was unable to see me for almost two months. And then one day, four weeks before we returned home, Sergeant Hutchinson strode into our office a different woman. Her hair was pulled back, her cheeks were rosy, and I think I saw a trace of lip gloss. She smiled brightly. I had never seen her smile before.

"Our unit has adopted this puppy," she started as she sat down. I had heard about several groups of Marines finding the orphaned puppies of wild dogs on base and making them unofficial mascots, feeding them with shipments of puppy chow sent from home. "Everybody liked him, but he always came to me. He sort of became mine. Anyway, I heard that some people were sending their puppies home —" My heart sank a little, immediately worried that my sensitive patient would be devastated if her plan did not succeed.

"So I came to talk to Major Loonan."

I smiled, proud of her initiative. "He's nice, isn't he?"

"Oh, ma'am, he is *so* nice," she gushed. "He took a look at Cocoa — that's what I'm calling him, 'cause he looks like the color of chocolate. Anyway, he gave him all his shots and did the operation to neuter him. And we did the worm medication, too. Major Loonan says he's in great health."

I had to admit I was surprised. Tim would not have gone to all that trouble if there were no chance of this woman being able to keep this dog, would he?

"He said he has a friend in Kuwait who would keep Cocoa for the six-week quarantine thing. He said I just needed to arrange to have him sent to Kuwait. So I went and talked to the C-130 squadron, and they said sure, they'd take him."

Patients rarely truly surprise me. I sat and stared at her.

"So Cocoa got to Kuwait, Major Loonan told me, and the vet there did all the customs paperwork and all that was left was an airline ticket. So my mom and dad got that, and they picked him up at the Detroit airport yesterday. They're going to bring him to San Diego for me when we get home." She sat back in her chair, crossed her arms over her chest, and grinned.

"Wow." I shook my head. "That is just wonderful news! I am very proud of you. And you must be very proud of yourself, too."

"I am, ma'am. You know how you kept telling me to start looking at the goals I had for my life once I get home? Like, to find the things I looked forward to?"

I nodded.

"Well, I figured out what they are. Cocoa came into my life for a reason. I have to take care of him now."

"Good for you."

"And I'm going to apply for the working dog program in the Marine Corps," she added. "I figure once you know what it is you love, you might as well do everything you can to fit it into every part of your life."

I believe good doctors learn from their patients every day. But I had never expected that in the middle of the desert half a world away, a female sergeant in the Marine Corps would define a new cure for depression.

HOME

On a blistering, windy August afternoon in Iraq, when even the wispiest cloud was a distant memory, my father wrote about rain.

> Yesterday was a typical summer afternoon in the South — hot and muggy. Toward evening it clouded up and before I knew it, everything was dark and a severe thunderstorm had moved in. The trees were bent over; the street was overflowing, even with those big culverts you have. Your mom and I assumed our usual places out on the lanai with the twins to enjoy the show. We all clapped for the bright flashes of light and the especially loud thunderclaps. This has become a regular summertime activity for us.
>
> Our technique appears to have worked, because when we picked up the kids one day last week after a particularly loud thunderstorm, their teacher told us that all the other kids were afraid of the noise and started crying — except Brian and Meg. The two of them apparently stood at the window and watched the storm, with smiles on their faces.

Have I told you lately that I love you? I do, and I am so very proud of what you are doing . . .

I sat for a moment, staring at my dad's words on the lap-top screen. My children, not even two years old, might never again in their lives be upset by the sound of thunder. I wondered if I would be able to say the same thing.

The Legend of the Camel Spider, Part II

On a scorching evening toward the end of our deployment, Katie entered the room Karen and I shared with her, holding her tiny digital camera. I looked up from my book.

"Look at my picture of what was in the shower this morning." She held up the camera so I could view the image. I inhaled sharply.

"Oh, shit . . . is that what I think it is?" We still had not actually seen one up close.

"Yep. Camel spider. As big as my hand. And I was only wearing shower shoes and a towel! Everyone over here was gone and I had no idea what to do, so I went next door to the guys."

"In your towel?"

"What was I going to do? I couldn't very well take a shower with that thing in there."

I couldn't argue with that.

"Bill was the only one there, and he came back over with me. But he had flip-flops on too. So we found a box in the dumpster. We picked the spider up and ran outside with it."

"Did it jump?"

"No, it just kind of sat there in the box."

"You let it go?" I was incredulous.

"Yeah," she said, forwarding her camera to the next picture. There was the huge creature in all its dirt-colored glory basking in the sand outside the front door of our barracks.

"What did it do?" I imagined the shade-seeking monster chasing Katie's and Bill's shadows at five miles per hour once they let it out of the box.

"Well, I think it might have been sick," she said thoughtfully. "It just sort of sauntered away."

"Sauntered."

"Right."

The Little Boy

As the days of deployment drew to a close, I found it more and more difficult to pray. I continued to attend Mass every Sunday without fail, but my quiet time alone with my God, from which I used to gain strength and find peace, seemed disconnected and distant. A person not often at a loss for words, I found myself speechless in my soul.

Over pancakes one morning in the middle of August, Jason told me about a patient he had seen several days before, a young Marine whose job was to man the big gun atop a vehicle. Gunners were widely known, at least in clinical anecdotes among medical personnel, as those most at risk in the entire combat environment.

"He was on a convoy recently," Jason told me. The syrup that morning was especially thick, settling around my pancake like a clear, tan-tinted frosting. I was determined, so I cut one piece with my fork and lightly dipped it in the blob. The actual granules of sugar were visible. I must have wrinkled my nose, because Jason smiled.

I moved on to powdered eggs, looking up at Jason. He was struggling with the pancakes as well.

"So their convoy moved through a little village," Jason went on. "The street was lined with kids who were throwing rocks or yelling insults."

Because many of the people of the Al Anbar province, in which we were stationed, were generally hostile to Americans, the Marines did not have the same opportunities as the Army did to see the waving and cheering Iraqis that were found in other regions of the country.

The Marine had told Jason that while he manned the gun, as they moved through the crowd of children, he saw a young boy, no older than five. The boy was holding a paper bag, scrunching the top closed in his fist.

While the Marine watched, the five-year-old child raised his arm back over his shoulder to throw the bag. Of course, children had been used in this exact manner before, taught to throw hand grenades or larger explosives, often hidden in paper bags, at convoys.

I lowered my fork and watched Jason, unblinking.

"He told me that protocol for him in that situation was crystal clear. His job was to neutralize the threat to the convoy."

I realized I was holding my breath, and exhaled.

"So he paused. Just for a moment," Jason said. "He paused, and that little boy threw that bag right at his Humvee."

I gulped.

"Nothing happened." Jason finished the story and took a bite. "The bag didn't have anything in it."

We lowered our heads simultaneously, looking at our unappetizing food with numb ambivalence.

"My God," I whispered.

Jason nodded. "He came to me distraught. He had put his convoy at tremendous risk with that split-second decision to wait. He took a chance, and maybe it was an involuntary decision. But that bag could have exploded and killed Marines, and possibly other kids on the road. He knew that. He also knew that he managed, in that split second, *not* to kill an unarmed child.

"What was I supposed to tell him? That he made the right choice? The wrong choice?" He shook his head and lowered his forehead to his hand.

"Can you believe that these sorts of absolutely insane situations face these people half our age every single day out here?" I asked him. "Do we actually, realistically, expect them to be able to cope with this and not have any complications?"

Jason did not have an answer for me. No one did, of course, but it did feel better to say it out loud.

"What did you do with the patient?" I asked.

"Just sat with him awhile. He talked some about guilt, and some about shame. He told me he needed to be sure of what decision he would make the next time."

"Did you send him back?"

"Of course." There were so few we did not. Despite their intense pain in situations just like this one, nearly to the man or woman, our U.S. Marine patients wanted to stay with their units.

"After all, he was fine," Jason mused. "Just needed to cry a little and figure it out, I guess."

"You cured him in one session." I grinned, trying to lighten the mood. Jason appreciated the effort, I could tell, but did not return my smile.

Jason's story followed me throughout my day of seeing patients, invading my thoughts whenever I had a moment of silence. I thought about his young patient, this warrior of eighteen who came face to face with a decision most people could never fathom. I was impressed with Jason's clinical acumen, as always, and his understanding that the Marine just needed to cry.

That night, as the brilliant red sun dipped below the desert horizon, I curled up on my cot in a modified fetal position. I did it on purpose. Hugging my knees and rocking slightly, I hoped that in this childlike posture I would *feel* something in conjunction with Jason's story. After all, I used to feel when I was a kid.

It didn't work. My limbs, my eyes, and my heart felt anesthetized.

"Heavenly Father," I began out loud, desperate. I paused. I wanted to ask Him to take care of Jason's patient and all other Marines in his role, and to comfort their aching hearts. I wanted to ask for His protection for the children of Iraq, keeping them out of harm's way. I wanted to ask Him to watch over our surgical and trauma teams and to help them some-day wash off the blood. I wanted to ask Him for strength for Jason, for our techs, and for me as we waded every day through the fear and grief of teenagers. I wanted to beg Him to guard Mike and my babies and bring me safely home to them.

I knew what I wanted to say. But the words eluded me — falling, unspoken and deadened, somewhere far away.

"Help," I whispered to the darkening room. I allowed my eyes to drift shut and sleep to overtake me.

I figured He knew what I meant.

HOME

I sat in the Internet café one evening in late August reading my father's daily e-mail account of life in hot, humid Florida. He and my mother were tired, he wrote, but their fatigue was their own doing. After all, they had been up late every night watching the Olympics.

The Olympics.

I pushed my chair back, away from the laptop, and stared at the screen. I had forgotten about the Olympics. Like most Americans, I loved watching our elite athletes compete against the rest of the world for gold. Seeing them graced with flowers and medals, tears streaming down their faces as they listened to "The Star-Spangled Banner," always made my heart swell with pride. They were their country's heroes in those moments.

Walking back to the barracks, I suddenly longed for the national anthem. I had not heard it played at all out here, with the exception of that one tape-recorded version played at the Seabees' memorial service.

I wondered about Corporal Dunham. If the investigation into his death concluded that he should be awarded the

Congressional Medal of Honor, a special ceremony would be held at the White House, "The Star-Spangled Banner" would play, and Jason Dunham's mother would cry. She would probably receive flowers, and she and his father would accept the beautiful light blue medal on their son's behalf. Would even a tiny fraction of Americans see the president bestow the nation's highest award?

I am certain that before I left for Iraq I had known this would be a Summer Olympics year. But I had allowed myself to forget. It was nothing against our athletes; I felt proud of them, as always.

They simply were not my heroes anymore.

The Last Patient

In the States, football season was under way. In Iraq, the only signs of autumn were high temperatures just under the summer's peaks of 132°F. Our seabags were ready to go. Our flight home was scheduled. Most important, the members of our replacement surgical company had arrived.

I set my radio and pistol on the desk in our small office, and HM2 Gob briefed me on the history of my final new patient in Iraq. We would turn the hospital over in several days. An air of excitement enlivened us as we marched through our final clinical days at Al Asad — as palpable as the fear and uncertainty that hovered around our replacements.

Gob introduced my patient and left the room, closing the door behind him.

The gunnery sergeant's arms stretched the fabric of his desert utility uniform taut. A pistol was strapped to his right thigh. His face was sunburned and his hair was light brown, graying at the temples, and closely cut in the Marine high and tight, the nickname for the standard Marine Corps haircut.

"Good morning, Gunnery Sergeant," I said, extending my hand.

"Morning, ma'am." He gripped my hand tightly and looked straight at me.

We both took a seat.

"Petty Officer Gob tells me you're experiencing some difficulty sleeping lately?"

"Yes, ma'am."

"Nightmares, too, I understand?"

He nodded.

"Any disturbing images you are unable to get out of your mind?"

"Yes, ma'am."

"What can you tell me about those?"

His light blue eyes appeared distant and glassy. He exhaled sharply and looked at the floor.

"I was standing in front of the exchange the night of the first attack," he started, his voice cracking. "When that first rocket came in, right next to us really, shrapnel hit several of my Marines. I remember I looked at Corporal Overton —" He paused and looked at me. I nodded. "And he was just lying there. He wasn't moving. I couldn't tell if he was breathing, but I knew it was bad — there was blood everywhere. I threw him over my shoulder and carried him to the hospital — it's about two hundred yards, but it felt like two miles. I yelled out for someone to help me, and a few corpsmen ran out, put him on a gurney, and took him inside." He screwed his eyes shut.

"What did you do when they took him inside?" I asked.

"I just sat there for a while. I didn't know what to do. It was so crazy, I felt like the only thing to do was to get back to my unit — so I left. I left him there, to —" His voice faltered. He swallowed hard and lowered his gaze.

I nodded again. I remembered.

I had seen Corporal Overton's body in the basement of the hospital that night, the first of many nights during which rockets pounded our base. His boots had been removed and were neatly placed at the edge of his gurney on the dusty and cracked tile floor.

A scratchy green wool blanket covered his body to his ankles, and his toes peeked out. A thick crimson stain spread across the floor from under his head. Upstairs, the boots of the living pounded on the tile, and voices yelled commands. Once it was determined that shrapnel from that rocket had penetrated Overton's brain and killed him instantly, someone had carried his body to the basement to make room for other injured patients. It was battlefield medicine. Triage demanded it. We hated it.

I refocused on the gunnery sergeant's face.

"I was doing fine for six months, ma'am. I didn't really even think about it once we buried Overton. But now, suddenly —" He extended both arms in front of him, making fists with his hands.

"I keep seeing pieces of his flesh on my uniform — and his blood is everywhere. It's all over me — and I can't get it off —"

He opened his hands and turned them up. He examined

his trembling fingers for a moment before lowering his elbows to his knees, and his face to his palms. He began to sob, his big shoulders shaking.

Pulling with the heels of my boots, I scooted my chair across the dusty floor until I was sitting squarely in front of the weeping Marine. In a gesture unlike anything I have ever done in a normal therapy situation, I reached out and touched his arm. He looked up.

I took both his hands in mine. There was nothing normal about this situation.

"I remember Corporal Overton, Gunnery Sergeant," I whispered to him. "We all do. His death touched us and we will never forget him."

He was the first Marine we had treated who was killed in action. How could we forget?

"I am so very sorry — for your loss."

He stared at me. We sat in silence, battling different gruesome images of the same young man's death.

"Thank you, ma'am," he finally breathed.

"What you're going through is a traumatic injury. What you endured that day, seeing your men injured seriously, carrying your Marine to the hospital — is not a normal human experience. And you dealt with it through denial for the last six months because you had to. You functioned and you did your job. Now it's time to pay attention to it. That's all. You are dreaming about him and seeing his blood again because your mind is trying to tell you — it's time."

He nodded, searching my face for reassurance that he was

not going insane. I smiled at him. He was still clutching my hands.

"You're going to be okay," I whispered.

In the beginning of my deployment, there were tears of loss. Today my eyes were dry. Early on, there was a deep ache in response to my patients' distress. Today, my nerves were deadened.

As a clinician, I knew that human beings develop coping mechanisms to adapt to chronic trauma. I realized that emotional numbness had become mine.

At least my patients could still cry.

Cheeseburgers,
Part II

On our last official day as the Combat Stress Platoon of Alpha Surgical Company, Jason and I joked to our psych techs that we would treat them to a delicious breakfast. Together, the four of us walked to the chow hall. Petty Officers Gob and Patacsil filled their trays and sat across from Jason and me at the long table. It was rare that the four of us sat together and looked at one another. We had simply been too busy.

A psychiatric technician is a specialized hospital corpsman in the Navy. During peacetime, he supports the psychiatrists and psychologists of his clinic. As a member of a combat stress platoon, however, the right Sailor has the opportunity to move far beyond a support role and take on the responsibility of direct patient care. Gob and Patacsil were the right Sailors. They not only directed our team's schedule, they conducted all of the histories for our new evaluations, carried therapy caseloads of their own, and managed all emergencies. During the entire seven-month deployment, I was paged to the hospital in the middle of the night only a few times. Gob or Patacsil always took care of things. In doing so, they took care of us.

Jason and I told our teammates that morning that we were

proud of them. We thanked them and said we couldn't have done it without them.

Gob and Patacsil simply shrugged. Just doing their jobs, they said.

Then the four of us got up from the table, dumped our trays, and hiked several miles across our sprawling base to the Mortuary Affairs compound, where we would conduct our last group therapy session as a team.

The Marines of MA had requested our return. As we all sat down, I marveled at how these same twenty-five faces around our circle looked so much calmer, so much older, and so much more exhausted than they had those many months ago.

When we first met these men, they had been afraid. But now, on this stifling Iraq morning in late August — three days before they left for home — they were angry.

They were angry that U.S. Marines had to die. They were angry that they were the ones to take care of mutilated bodies. They were angry that no one understood what they experienced. They expressed concern about what they should share with their families. They worried about traumatizing others.

Finally, and most significant, they were angry — grieving, actually, although they did not realize it — that their unit was being split up to return home. They had been pulled from many different commands for this deployment. Now, as they were about to say good-bye, they realized their only solace had been in one another. The men sat around the circle that morning with the only other people in the world who understood.

During our session, they made arrangements for their first reunion, for e-mail correspondence to a group list, and for a standing plan to check in on everyone. This was most certainly second best to being sent home as a unit and to staying together, but it was the best they could do.

The four of us left them that morning and walked back to our barracks in silence. Although the Marines of MA had performed their jobs with honor and learned the value in trusting one another, we worried about them. They were a special group out here, exposed to chronic and unrelenting trauma. And now they were being split up, each facing the future alone.

We wondered if others might say the same thing about us.

Drowning

I dreamed about camel spiders a lot. They reared and hissed and ran and jumped all around my subconscious. This particular night in late August, I dreamed I was trying to nudge one out of our barracks room with a shovel. The strategy was not working.

The next moment, our windows rattled and the walls trembled and the foundation rocked with such force and sheer volume that I physically fell out of my cot. I landed with a jolt on the concrete deck, instantly awake. Reaching under my cot, I grabbed my helmet and clumsily strapped it on.

"Shit!" Karen screamed from across the room. She and Katie were also getting into flak jackets and helmets. The explosions came fast and loud, as if encircling our barracks.

"We are going home in one week, you assholes," I said loudly to the windows. "One week. Do you hear me?" The next crack sounded farther away. From her cot next to me, Cat grinned.

"Ooh-rah, ma'am."

"Cat, what will I do without you?"

The rockets stopped. The four of us got up and walked to

the head at the end of the passageway. We all wore either workout clothing or scrubs — with flak jackets and helmets, of course.

Our watches read 0510. The women of our company stood sleepily outside their doors, waiting for the all-clear call and the accountability report from the hospital. The women of the replacement company huddled together in one corner, white and trembling. This was their first attack.

Today, the hospital would be entirely theirs. We would turn over responsibility to them at 0700.

None of us could return to sleep, so we started talking. Katie had been on duty last night to train the new ward nurses. When we asked her about her night, her expression remained stone-cold. Karen, Cat, and I sat on her cot around her, figuring she needed to talk.

She did.

Last night, on its last official day of responsibility, Alpha Surgical Company lost its first patient on the operating table.*

Three casualties had come in at 2200. Two of them were stabilized in the SST. Both trauma teams, ours and the new group's, were there, making for a lot of medical people in the room, but also for a lot of experience.

One of the three patients was critical. He had been shot in the abdomen. Katie said that he came into the SST talking. He

---

*Until that night, all of our surgery patients had been stabilized and medevaced to Baghdad.

said his name was John. She held his hand and told him she was there. He kept his eyes locked on hers, and she told him not to give up. As the team worked to stabilize his wounds, his blood volume dropped and he was taken to the OR. Katie said she noticed his eyes go dull at that moment. She knew he had stopped fighting.

She took a deep, shuddering breath and continued her story.

He was raced to the OR, but his vitals began dropping dramatically while the chest tube was being placed. The OR team worked on and on but could not stop the bleeding. John died just after 2300. At 0300, Katie returned to our barracks to try to sleep.

We looked at Katie. Her expression was frozen, a pale mask of numb shock. Karen held her hand.

"Our last night. Our last patient. I watched him give up. I watched him die. There was nothing we could do. I am done. I am done with this."

Karen scooted over and wrapped an arm around Katie's shoulder. Katie rested her head on Karen's shoulder, her eyes staring straight ahead, unblinking.

Later that morning, Debbie, our nurse anesthetist, approached me and asked if we could talk. Her bloodshot eyes told the story before she did. She said the OR staff appeared to be struggling over John's death the night before, and she asked me to talk to them.

Debbie and I spoke for a few minutes. She expressed the same grief and frustration I had heard from Katie. She told me she felt out of control.

"I told the OR team that the patient's pulse was forty-five," she remembered. "Then, about ten seconds later, I told them it was thirty-seven. The chest tube was almost in, and I looked up and it was twenty-seven. It was the next second that I didn't have a pulse. I yelled at everyone that I didn't have a pulse — I kept saying it over and over again — there's blood all over the floor, he's bleeding out —"

She exhaled and bowed her head. I sat quietly with her in the shade of the building and waited. We sat together in silence for several minutes. Finally, she nodded at me, got up, and walked to her tiny room in the hospital, head down.

Over the next few hours I talked with several of the company's OR techs, the corpsmen who assist the surgeons. As the morning wore on, I heard the same story — about John talking, telling them his name and what happened when he was shot, his heart rate dropping, his suddenly bleeding out, his dying in front of their eyes.

When everyone was through talking at last, I headed back to the barracks. I sat down on my cot, unstrapped my holster, and laid my pistol next to me. I took in a deep breath and released it slowly. The next breath felt shallow and tight. I immediately struggled against it.

Suddenly, I was overcome by a sensation of actual drowning. My lungs burned and my breathing shortened and thinned. The few colors in the room around me turned to gray. I felt there was absolutely no way I could tread water for one single moment more before I went under.

Thankfully, I did not have to. The mini–panic attack passed as soon as I realized the reason for it. I was allowed to feel everything at once. Alpha Surgical Company and the medical care of the U.S. Marines in western Iraq belonged in other hands as of 0700 today.

It was over.

HOME

Kristen, one of my dearest friends from the Navy, married the love of her life over Labor Day weekend. All of the girls who had been inseparable since our time in flight surgeon school drank champagne together at her wedding in Virginia, except for me; I sat in a dusty Internet café in the middle of the desert. An e-mail from Margy described the fantastic night.

At one point during the evening, Kristen and Dino got up and took the mike. They made a toast, asking everyone to raise their glasses in a tribute to their two friends who could not be at the wedding because they were serving their country. One of them, they said, was flying Hornets off a carrier in the Persian Gulf, and the other was caring for U.S. Marines in western Iraq.

There was not a dry eye at our table. We are all so proud of you, Heidi.

You were missed.

The List

In some ways, this early September morning was a carbon copy of every other morning in Iraq. I arrived at Jason's room just after 0730, and we walked to breakfast together amid rapidly increasing temperatures. But today was different. For the first time in more than seven months, there was no 0700 OIC morning meeting to attend before I retrieved Jason. Those meetings were over. Our replacements were in charge of the hospital now.

Jason, Bill, Steve, and I planned to watch the final episode of *The Sopranos* that night. For 220-something days, every Tuesday and Sunday night we escaped to the violent and humorous world of that endearing HBO New Jersey crime family and salivated as they ate delicious-looking Italian food on screen. When we first arrived in Iraq, we carefully planned a schedule to ensure that we would view the finale on the night before we went home. Finale night had arrived at last.

Jason and I rounded the corner from our barracks onto the long, narrow road to the chow hall. Countless people in tan utility uniforms with rifles over their shoulders or pistols strapped to their legs moved in both directions around us. As we navigated around holes in the broken concrete, a group of Marines passed on my right and I said good morning. Several of them shouted in response, "Ooh-rah, ma'am!"

I had to smile.

"Aren't you going to miss that?" I asked Jason.

"Miss what?"

"As we walk to the chow hall each day, nearly every person who passes by says 'good morning' or 'ooh-rah' to us. You have to admit, there aren't many places where that happens."

"Any Marine base in the world, Heidi."

"You know what I mean. It is really cool. I'm going to miss it."

"Okay," said Jason wryly, grinning sideways at me.

"I think I'm going to write a list," I announced as we reached the chow hall and got in line. "It'll have two columns — things that were good about Iraq and things that were bad."

Jason and I stepped up to the line of sinks in the chow line and turned on the water.

"That will be a pretty lopsided list, don't you think?" he asked, squirting a large amount of industrial-strength hand soap into his hands.

"Sure." I ripped a piece of paper towel from a gigantic roll. "But I'm going to do it anyway. For instance, Marines saying 'ooh-rah' as I walk to chow; that's something good about Iraq. I think it'll be good therapy for me. Call it closure."

We each asked for pancakes and two hard-boiled eggs. That morning I realized that Jason and I had eaten pancakes every single morning for more than seven months. Of course, on those happy occasions when the food trucks brought fresh eggs, we considered it a great treat to add the hard-boiled eggs to our trays.

Over the course of our deployment, we often commented on good-egg days, on which our eggs peeled easily and the whites looked smooth and perfect, and bad-egg days, which usually involved an inordinate amount of time peeling tiny cracked pieces of shell and ending up with a mangled mess of an egg.

This was a good-egg day.

With no responsibilities at the hospital, Karen and I went to the gym in the late morning and then returned to our room to watch a few episodes of *Sex and the City*. She then donned her headphones, stretched out on her cot, and began writing in her journal. I started typing my list. It was easier than I imagined.

I walked to the Internet café that night and sent the list home with an accompanying e-mail to a few family members and friends.

We are almost on our way. The good news is that we depart in the middle of the night and arrive (all admin tasks complete, including turning our weapons in to the armory!) around dinnertime at Camp Pendleton — on the same day we leave. The other good news is it appears we have commercial air carriers taking us home, so we don't have to worry about sleeping on the cold steel deck of an Air Force C-17.

We turned over authority of the surgical company to our replacements, who had a serious trial by fire here in multiple ways, including casualties, surgeries, increased risk to their personal safety, power outages, water outages, and camel spiders in the hospital — all in their first four days. But yesterday, we heard the helicopters coming and knew they were dealing with the traumas. And we sat in our barracks and waited for them to call us if they needed us. They never did.

I decided one of the things I should compose for my own closure and healing was a list: Things That Were Good about Iraq and being deployed with the Marines, and Things That Were Not Good. My hope is that somehow the trauma, the fear, the grief, the laughter, the pride, and the patriotism that have marked this long seven months for me will begin to make sense through my writing.

So, here goes . . .

THINGS THAT WERE GOOD
Sunset over the desert . . . almost always orange
Sunrise over the desert . . . almost always red
The childlike excitement of having fresh fruit at dinner after going weeks without it

Being allowed to be the kind of clinician I know I can be, and want to be, with no limits placed and no doubts expressed

But most of all,
The United States Marines, our patients . . .

Walking, every day, and having literally every single person who passed by say "Ooh-rah, Ma'am . . ."

Having them tell us, one after another, through blinding pain or morphine-induced euphoria . . . "When can I get out of here? I just want to get back to my unit . . ."

Meeting a young Sergeant, who had lost an eye in an explosion . . . he asked his surgeon if he could open the other one . . . when he did, he sat up and looked at the young Marines from his fire team who were being treated for superficial shrapnel wounds in the next room . . . he smiled, lay back down, and said, "I only have one good eye, Doc, but I can see that my Marines are OK."

And of course, meeting the one who I will never forget . . . the one who threw himself on a grenade to save the men at his side . . . who will likely be the first Medal of Honor recipient in over 11 years . . .

My friends . . . some of them will be life-long in a way that is inde-scribable
My patients . . . some of them had courage unlike anything I've ever experienced before

My comrades, Alpha Surgical Company . . . some of the things wit-nessed will traumatize them forever, but still they provided outstand-ing care to these Marines, day in and day out, sometimes for days at a time with no break, for 7 endless months

And finally, above all else . . .
Holding the hand of that dying Marine

THINGS THAT WERE NOT GOOD

Terrifying camel spiders, poisonous scorpions, flapping bats in the darkness, howling, territorial wild dogs, flies that insisted on landing on our faces, giant, looming mosquitoes, invisible sand flies that carry leishmaniasis

132 degrees
Wearing long sleeves, full pants, and combat boots in 132 degrees
Random and totally predictable power outages that led to sweating throughout the night
Sweating in places I didn't know I could sweat . . . like wrists, and ears

The roar of helicopters overhead
The resounding thud of exploding artillery in the distance
The popping of gunfire . . .
Not knowing if any of the above sounds is a good thing, or bad thing
The siren and the inevitable "big voice" yelling at us to take cover . . .
Not knowing if that siren was on someone's DVD or if the big voice would soon follow

The cracking sound of giant artillery rounds splitting open against rock and dirt
The rumble of the ground . . .
The shattering of the windows . . .
Hiding under flak jackets and Kevlar helmets, away from the broken

windows, waiting to be told we can come to the hospital . . . to treat the ones who were not so lucky . . .

Watching the black helicopter with the big red cross on the side landing at our pad
Worse . . . watching gray Marine helicopters filled with patients landing at our pad . . . because we usually did not realize they were coming . . .

Ushering a sobbing Marine Colonel away from the trauma bay while several of his Marines bled and cried out in pain inside

Meeting that 21-year-old Corporal with three Purple Hearts . . . and listening to him weep because he felt ashamed of being afraid to go back
Telling a room full of stunned Marines in blood-soaked uniforms that their comrade, that they had tried to save, had just died of his wounds

Trying, as if in total futility, to do anything I could, to ease the trauma of group after group . . . that suffered loss after loss, grief after inconsolable grief . . .

Washing blood off the boots of one of our young nurses while she told me about the one who bled out in the trauma bay . . . and then the one she had to tell, when he pleaded for the truth, that his best friend didn't make it . . .

Listening to another of our nurses tell of the Marine who came in talking, telling her his name . . . about how she pleaded with him not to give up, told him that she was there for him . . . about how she could see his eyes go dull when he couldn't fight any longer . . .

And finally, above all else . . .
Holding the hand of that dying Marine

The Watch

And then, just like that, it was time to go home.

Despite the fact that moving units to and from deployment in stages is routine practice in the military, it was shocking to witness half our surgical company pack up and depart Iraq a full week before the rest of us. The first group included Jason, Steve, Bill, and Cat. Seeing them off was strange and familiar at once, a surreal extension of the entire deployment—painful and a little funny, with an overarching numbness that pervaded all else. I wore sunglasses as I helped them load their seabags into the truck. I think I expected myself to cry.

Someone took a picture of Jason and me, my arm entwined with his. He didn't smile; I tried my best. We walked together toward the bus, exchanging pleasantries about safe travel and seeing each other when we were back at Camp Pendleton to turn in our sweat-stained flak jackets and that mosquito netting we never used.

We hugged briefly and he turned to walk away. Finding no words of my own, I blurted out a line I think I remembered from the series finale of *M*A*S*H*. One last time, their writers spoke for me.

"Jason," I said. He looked back. "I don't know what I would have done..." My voice caught in my throat. "...if I'd come to Iraq and not found you here."

He smiled, almost indiscernibly, and tipped his floppy hat to me. Bill and Steve were waiting for him. Together they trudged up the steps, and then they leaned out the windows and waved as the buses pulled away.

A peculiar sensation washed over me. I felt an intense urge to run to my little office in the hospital and begin seeing patients. If I could do that, I thought, I would feel needed, valuable, not so lost.

A group of us stood together watching until the buses were out of sight, wordlessly looking toward the front hatch of Alpha Surgical Company and at one another. *They all feel the same way*, I mused. *I am not the only one floundering here. This might be the longest week of our lives.*

A Blackhawk roared overhead and turned base to the hospital's landing pad. We craned our necks to watch as it landed in a veil of dust. We waited, but no one came out the front door of the hospital to ask for our help, and after a few minutes, we dispersed without a word.

The next morning was Sunday, and Karen, Katie, and I went to mass. The priest who had deployed with us had already departed; his replacement was a tall, dignified-looking man with a graying mustache. After the readings, he stood up in front of his new congregation to give the sermon, holding note cards in his hands.

He surveyed the several hundred sweaty, dirty faces that

looked at him with hollow stares. He put down his notes. He paused a few minutes in silence before he finally spoke.

"Wow. Well, look at all of you. You sure do look tired—really. Just exhausted."

People began shifting nervously in their seats. He went on.

"But here's the deal, folks. It just occurred to me that it's possible no one has told you this. So I will.

"You have done your duty." He articulated every word slowly.

"This was a tough time to be out here. A lot of bad things happened on your watch, and despite all that, you pulled together and overcame it all, and you did a really good job. We are proud to be taking over for you. But it is important that you understand one thing. We *are* taking over for you. We are here now.

"You can go home. You can let go. We have the watch."

A soundless sob stuck in my throat, and I turned to Karen. We grabbed hands. She felt it too.

It would take me years to finally understand what he did in that moment. He gave us, in our language, permission to depart. Someone else had the watch at last. We could not only go home, we could leave Iraq behind.

Or at least we could try.

The Beginning,
Part II

The men and women of Alpha Surgical Company returned as a unit to Camp Pendleton on a chartered (and patriotically decorated) American Airlines jet. Mike came to San Diego to meet us and cohosted a homecoming celebration with my sister, Steph, and my dear friends Alli, Margy, and Colette. I moved, trancelike, through the wonderful party, frankly stunned at every turn by everyday details: fresh air, fragrant tropical flowers, and colorful hot-air balloons that hovered over Alli's backyard. Color and sweet smells; two things that Iraq simply did *not* have.

Mike returned to Florida after the party, and my comrades and I spent eight days returning gear and attending debriefs at Pendleton. The majority of people from Alpha Surgical Company belonged to the naval hospital in San Diego. I had spent seven months telling Marines it would be important for their mental health to stay together as a unit upon return.

And then, after all my gear was turned in and my party was a memory, I boarded a plane by myself to return to Florida.

My husband, my children, and my parents met me at the

airport. In my neighborhood in Jacksonville, yellow ribbons embraced our trees and mailboxes. A huge silk-screened American flag that said WELCOME HOME, MOMMY hung over my front door.

I was home.

Before returning to the hospital, I took three weeks of leave. Over the next six months before I left active duty, I struggled to reconnect with my family; jumped at every car backfire, popped balloon, and firework; lost my appetite and ten more pounds; and battled bizarre nightmares.

Through it all, my return to seeing regular patients at Naval Hospital Jacksonville could only be described as torture.

My first day back in clinic after leave, I found myself sitting at my desk at 0730, staring blankly at a stack of charts that contained six new evaluations. After providing patient care every day of the week for seven months, I now felt strangely out of practice and incompetent.

While I procrastinated going out to meet my first patient, a large metal storage rack that was being moved on the floor above us crashed to the deck. The sound was deafening, a terrible crack of metal and concrete that caused my window to shudder in its sill.

I froze.

My heart seized. I clutched the medical chart I was holding so tight that my fingers blanched. I darted looks out my window at the blue fall sky and up at my white ceiling. I stood and walked to my open doorway, looking into the hall for signs that anyone else had heard the crash. Our doctors, corpsmen, and admin staff moved through their morning routines as if nothing had slammed into the ceiling above our heads. I bit my lip, battling tears of frustration. I knew it was just me. I knew it was the war, still with me.

HM3 Betancourt, a relatively junior psychiatric technician who had deployment experience with the Marines, saw me in the doorway and stopped. He moved toward me cautiously.

"Hey, ma'am. You okay?"

"Oh, sure," I said, not making eye contact and moving back

into my office, looking at my feet. He followed me, closing the door behind him.

"Dr. Kraft?"

I looked up.

"It's okay if you're not okay."

Two big tears slid down my face.

"I'm not," I whispered, sinking to the couch my patients used and covering my face with my hands.

HM3 Betancourt sat in my chair.

"I know, ma'am."

Ten minutes and very few words later, I shook his hand and strode out my door to wash my face and then retrieve my first patient from our waiting room.

And so I returned to life as a clinical psychologist in a peacetime hospital. Despite my clinical knowledge that each individual's suffering is real and important, I often found myself openly staring in disbelief at patients. I could not fathom the crises that my patients made out of their life events, nor could I empathize with the petty relationship, work, or financial stressors that brought them to tears in my office.

Only months before, I had held the hand of a twenty-two-year-old hero who gave his life to save two of his men. I had witnessed courage in the face of injury and pain, loyalty in the face of grief. Everyday psychological problems not only paled in comparison, they struck me as frankly absurd. Despite the personal toll seven months of war had taken, I found myself wishing I worked on a Marine base. At least then I would know what to say to my patients.

Over the months, I spoke with HM1 Botkin, our Leading Petty Officer in the psychiatry department, about some of my conflicts. When the referral to treat Corporal Paulsen came across his desk, he did not hesitate over which psychologist to assign. To this day, I appreciate his insight — he knew that not only did this patient need me, I needed him.

Corporal Paulsen's battalion was still in Iraq when he came to my care. He had been injured several weeks before and was sent home by medevac. He was allowed to visit family on leave, and his doctor asked us to look after him during that time. In her consult she stated that the corporal displayed total paralysis of his legs — with no medical indication for it whatsoever.

When I entered the waiting room at our first appointment, the young man with the blond high and tight saw my dark green Marine Corps utilities and desert boots, wheeled forward, and shook my hand firmly.

"You have no idea how great it is to see that uniform, ma'am," he said with a grin.

We entered my office together. Knowing that I would need to start slowly, I pulled my chair up next to his wheelchair and leaned back. Before I spoke, I noticed that he was looking at the pictures from the war on my bulletin board. Most were of people — Bill, Steve, Jason, Katie, Karen, and Cat.

One, taken by Bill, beautifully framed the decrepit mosque on our base within multiple circles of razor wire. The corporal seemed focused on that one. I waited.

"That's Al Asad!" he exclaimed. I nodded. He looked at me.

"So, ma'am . . . you were there."

"I was there."

He knew that his doctors could find no objective reason for his inability to move his legs. "It's called conversion disorder," he told me expertly. "I guess it means that my mind is fucking with my legs."

I smiled. He was right. That was exactly what it meant.

He started talking. He told me of the closeness of his unit and of his tremendous guilt about being home while they still fought in Iraq. He told stories of literal hand-to-hand combat, of the day he killed a man with his Ka-Bar when he was too close to use his rifle. He described the day he was shot.

"We were on the roof of a building. I was standing next to my lieutenant. I don't really know what happened, just this huge impact. And I fell."

"Off the top of the building?"

"Yes, ma'am. A bunch of rubble fell on top of me, and I was pinned. My rifle fell away during the fall, and when I could see through the dust, I realized I was stuck and couldn't reach it. I couldn't actually see the bad guys, but I knew they'd be coming soon."

I stared. "What happened?"

"I yelled up to my platoon to get their asses down there — and they yelled back for me to hold tight. It was pretty fucking scary, ma'am — pardon my language, ma'am."

"No problem. So obviously they got down to you."

"Yeah, they did. You know what's amazing? You know the body armor we wear? It stopped two AK-47 slugs. They're actually stuck in the plate. I asked if I could have it back, and they said I could."

"That is amazing." I made a note to go back to that story another time. I noticed that his skin was graying and beads of sweat forming on his forehead.

"Anyway, I guess I passed out, because the next thing I remember was the CASH."*

---

*Combat Surgical Hospital, run by the Army.

"No damage to your spinal cord? After a fall and having something land on you that was heavy enough to actually pin you."

"That's what the MRI says, ma'am. See for yourself. They sent it. Says my back, legs, neck — everything — are fine. Guess it's just my head that needs help."

"You know, combat can be really traumatic. People who have been through it sometimes experience a slow recovery from that trauma. It's pretty normal."

"Yeah, but most of them don't end up in a wheelchair, do they, ma'am?" He smirked at me. "I figure my body is trying to tell me something — now it's up to you to figure out what that is."

I smiled at him, stood up, shook his hand, and held the door open for the wheelchair. "Actually, that's up to you. I'm just here to watch it happen."

Corporal Paulsen came to see me three times a week for the next six weeks in conjunction with his physical therapy appointments and with my long list of things to do before I left active duty in the Navy. I spent the first several meetings listening, hoping to gain his trust.

And then, one day, he told me.

"A good friend of mine from when I was a kid — everyone called him Mule 'cause he was stubborn and ornery — anyway, he shows up at my battalion right before we left for Iraq. I couldn't believe it. He asked me what I'd been up to since graduation, and I said I'd joined the Marines. He said he'd joined the Navy. He was our corpsman. You know, don't you, ma'am — how we feel about our docs?"

I nodded.

His eyes misted over, but he went on. "Mule and I were always together, from that moment on. We were best friends. We carried each other's letters* when we went in country."

He bowed his head. I knew we were getting somewhere. The usually effusive corporal now visibly struggled to find and express his thoughts.

I waited through a long silence. At last, he looked up, but not at me. Glassy and unfocused, his eyes appeared thousands of miles away as he spoke.

"One day, we were on patrol. I was on point, and behind me were the LT, Mule, and another Marine. We approached a brick wall, where we waited while another fire team entered a building. They immediately took fire from bad guys on the roof who were shooting down at them. One of them was hit, and someone yelled, 'Corpsman up!' "

He inhaled deeply and seemed to hold his breath. I watched him.

"Mule came around the lieutenant and grabbed me by the shoulders, pulling me back and rounding the corner in front of me, not giving me a chance to cover him while he ran for the building.

---

*Letters to their next of kin, common items to give to someone else for safekeeping during combat.

"The guys on the roof lit him up. They shot him twenty-five times while I watched. When we finally carried his body to the helo, I could see daylight through him. He had this surprised look on his face. I closed his eyes so I wouldn't have to look at them anymore."

He sighed deeply. Big tears lingered in his eyes. I reached out and placed one hand on top of his, breaking my own rule — again.

"I'm so sorry — for the loss of your friend," I whispered.

"Thank you, ma'am."

We sat in silence together. I did not speak another word and let him cry.

Two days later we met again.

"That was pretty intense last time," he started.

"Yes."

"I haven't told anyone that story. It felt good to tell you."

"Have you thought any more about what it might mean?"

"Like what?"

"Well, I was thinking about you and Mule. And I was wondering — what feelings do you have now about his death? Other than grief at the loss of your friend?"

"Anger, I guess."

"Go on."

"Well, I'm pissed off that he didn't let me cover him. I'm pissed off at the bad guys for killing him. Mostly, I'm pissed off that there was nothing I could do."

I nodded. "Anything else?"

"Guilt."

"Why guilt?"

"It should have been me."

I waited.

"I mean, I was point. I should have gone first."

"And if you had gone first?"

"Mule would be alive. He'd be the one delivering my letter to my mom."

"Tell me — if Mule had *not* gone around you, if he had waited for your signal, what would you have done next?"

"I would have moved my team out, around the corner."

"How would you have moved out?"

"Ma'am?"

"What would you have done, physically, to move out?"

"Well, it's called a creep, kind of like a walk-run, which we do when we're moving around with weapons. I'm not sure if you've ever seen it —"

"Sure. And this walk-run, what exactly does it involve? What is the logical progression of the parts of your body in order to creep?"

"I would have just stepped forward, ma'am. I would have taken two or three steps forward, and they would have killed me."

"Right. Two or three steps forward. How?"

"With my feet."

"Exactly."

He looked at his motionless legs, and then at me. A slight smile crept onto his face.

Four days later, I cut through the pharmacy on my way to the psychiatric ward. As I approached the hospital's main passageway, the raucous cheer of many voices filled the air. I rounded the corner and froze in my tracks.

Corporal Paulsen was walking. He had exited the door of physical therapy with a walker, flanked by therapists, PT techs, and his mother. Just before he saw me, he had released his hands from the handles and taken a step unassisted.

I drew in my breath. He grinned widely.

"Hey, ma'am! Look at me."

"Look at you, Marine. You are a sight for sore eyes." I felt my smile spread across my entire face.

"I guess my wheelchair had a purpose for a while — but it doesn't seem to anymore."

"Sure looks that way to me."

He would survive. His experience would always be with him, and he would survive in spite of it. Even, some days, because of it.

And so would I.

"Ma'am?"

"Yes, Corporal?"

He extended his hand. I stepped forward and shook it.

"Thank you."

"That's what I'm here for."

After all, I wore the uniform of a Medical Service Corps officer in the United States Navy. And during times of war, those of us in this uniform took care of our Marines. That statement went both ways.

It always has.

HEIDI KRAFT

Epilogue

On November 10, 2006 (the 231st birthday of the U.S. Marine Corps and what would have been Corporal Jason Dunham's twenty-fifth birthday), President Bush announced that Corporal Dunham would be posthumously awarded the Congressional Medal of Honor. On January 11, 2007, I had the distinct honor of attending the ceremony at the White House, as a guest of Corporal Dunham's parents, when the president awarded the medal to his family.

It stands alone as the single proudest day of my life.

ACKNOWLEDGMENTS

From the bottom of my heart, thank you . . .

To Mike, to Brian, and to Megan: for going on without me and for making me whole when I returned. All of this, everything I did and everything I ever will do, is for you.

To Bill and Bette Squier, my dad and mom: for the monumental sacrifice of love you made for your daughter and your grandchildren. Everything was immensely more bearable knowing you were there, loving them.

To my sister, Steph: for the greatest care packages ever sent; for your love and concern; and for the DVDs of my children — my lifeline, although I didn't realize how much until I returned home.

To the entire extended family, both Squier and Kraft sides: for your unified show of support for Mike and me.

To Hunter, Nisha, and Captain Goldberg . . . friends, mentors, OIF I vets: for being the only ones, at the time, who understood.

To Margy, Kristen, Mary, Colette, Alli, Joni, Katja, Tanya, Paula, Kelly, Deb, Cindy, Karen, Bith, Heather, Martin, Cowboy, Kim, Rick, Stephanie, Lori, Christi, Jill, Mental, Stork, Diane, Beret, Gary, Buster, Deke, Whymee, the people of the Mental Health Department at NH Jax — my friends: for the letters, packages, e-mails, and prayers that kept me going.

ACKNOWLEDGMENTS

To Lieutenant Colonel Otto Lehrack, USMC (ret.): for immediately knowing the real me after reading, "The List," for finding me, encouraging me, unrelentingly convincing me to write it all down; for helping the work come to life in such a real way; and most of all, for believing in me.

To Stu Miller, former Marine and agent extraordinaire: for your patience and guidance through a completely foreign process to me, and for crying with me the day it was announced that Corporal Dunham would be awarded the Medal of Honor.

To Liz Nagle, my wonderful editor: for your fantastic ideas and your uncanny ability to know how my writing will sound so much better; for your ability to laugh with me.

To Michael Phillips, *Wall Street Journal* reporter and author of *A Gift of Valor:* for so beautifully telling Jason Dunham's story to the world, and for holding my hand during Deb's speech at Quantico.

To Karen Guenther; Lieutenant General Chip Gregson, USMC (ret.); and everyone at the Injured Marine Semper Fi Fund: for your unfailing support of our country's heroes.

To Captain Koffman, another OIF I vet: for checking up on us at Al Asad. It did matter to us, very much.

To Petty Officers (then) Gob, Patacsil, and Blythe: for taking care of us and all those Marines.

To Jen: for your friendship and laughter and the "Eye in the sky" song.

To Katie: for keeping us motivated, for your positive attitude, for holding John's hand as he died.

To Paul: for listening, for caring, for being there, and for giving me a new appreciation of the Doors.

ACKNOWLEDGMENTS

To Steve: for being the one who woke up that night I stumbled to your room at 0300 with heat exhaustion and palpitations, for letting me sleep on your floor, for adjusting my spine once a week for seven months, and for your infectious grin.

To Cat: for being the Marine we all looked to. We still do. Ooh-rah.

To Bill (aka "The Hammer"): for making me laugh, for sharing your music, for organizing *Sopranos* nights, and for calling me your Mini-Hammer and your friend.

To Karen: for your fabulous laugh, for your wonderful, supportive friendship in the desert and ever since. I am so proud of you.

To Jason: for your empathy, your unending support, and for being the best partner I could ever ask for. I very honestly do not know what I would have done if I had arrived in Iraq and not found you there. This book is for Rhys, too. Maybe someday they'll all understand. Maybe someday we'll understand.

And finally, to Deb, Dan, Justin, Kyle, and Katie Dunham: for inviting me into your lives and for the once-in-a-lifetime experience of being with you as Corporal Jason Dunham was awarded the Medal of Honor; for believing that he heard my voice when I begged him to keep fighting; for knowing in your hearts that he did.

". . . the cherished memory of the loved and lost, and the solemn pride that must be yours to have laid so costly a sacrifice upon the altar of freedom."

— President Abraham Lincoln, 1864

About the Author

Heidi Squier Kraft received her PhD in clinical psychology from the San Diego University / University of California, San Diego, Joint Doctoral Program in Clinical Psychology in 1996. She joined the Navy during internship and served as both a flight and a clinical psychologist. In February 2004, when her twin boy and girl were fifteen months old, she deployed to Iraq for seven months with a Marine Corps surgical company. She left active duty in 2005 after nine years in the Navy and now serves as the deputy coordinator for the U.S. Navy Combat Stress Control Program. She lives in San Diego with her husband and children.

Reading Group Guide

RULE NUMBER TWO

Lessons I Learned
in a Combat Hospital

by

DR. HEIDI SQUIER KRAFT

A conversation with Dr. Heidi Squier Kraft

What inspired you to write Rule Number Two *upon your return to the United States?*

"The List," which I share in the book, was sent home to a small group of family and friends via e-mail. By the time I returned home in September 2004, "The List" had literally been forwarded around the world. It led to many people getting in touch with me, including medical personnel and Marines from the Vietnam and Korean Wars, and even WWII. It was overwhelming and humbling, as many of them told me the list made them remember—and that remembering was a good thing.

One of those Marines was retired infantry colonel Otto Lehrack, author of several books about the Marines in Vietnam. He told me that, in his opinion, every line in the poem needed to be a chapter in a book. At the time, I had no intention of writing anything else about the experience. But as the months went on and my transition home proved difficult and painful, I turned to writing (just as I had in Iraq) as a healing and therapeutic process. Otto helped me edit chapters as they were written; I had no idea they would one day become public.

One year and 250 pages later, I emerged myself again, and the journey was complete. My therapy was finished. Along the way I sent the chapter about Jason Dunham to his mother. She told me that the mothers of America needed to know these stories, and she asked me to consider submitting the book for publication. I can't say no to her, so—with the help of a terrific agent who is also a Marine—here we are.

The news of your deployment was sudden—you were given just eleven days to ready yourself and your family for your departure, and a further week to train for war at Camp Pendleton. What most surprised you when you reached Iraq? What could no one have prepared you for?

We were all surprised by the number of U.S. casualties for which we provided care, during the battle for Fallujah and throughout our entire deployment. There was no way to know what was in store for us with regard to sheer numbers and types of injuries.

No one could ever have prepared me for what it would be like to sit with, and do my best to comfort, an American Marine while he was dying, once we had been forced through the necessity of battlefield medicine to admit there was nothing we could do to save his life. Those were and still are some of the most horrible and wonderful moments of my life—at the same time.

You discuss the impasse you reached when you realized that in order to function and survive, you would need to redirect your caretaking impulse from your children to the soldiers. This must have been extremely difficult. How did you do it?

Every one of us is capable of the unimaginable in a situation that demands it. There was no other alternative for me.

What was it like being a woman on the base? Do you think your experience differed greatly from Bill's and Jason's? What advice would you offer women embarking on similar missions?

We were in the vast minority on our particular base. That said, I always felt protected by and cared for by my male comrades and friends, as well as the Marines who watched over us. I am quite certain that our experiences as women and mothers differ from those of our male counterparts, although it is difficult to say why in a qualitative way. I think that mothers share a guilt about leaving their children that seems universal in all whom I have had the privilege to meet since my return from war.

I hope that all female service members, and especially those with children, will be able to give themselves permission to be gone, to perform their service to their country with pride, and to forgive themselves for being away.

On several occasions you mention the great difficulty of sharing your daily life in Iraq with your family and friends back home. How did the bond you formed with your colleagues develop as a result? Are you still close to them now?

The movie *Band of Brothers* is named that for a reason. The experience of combat is an intense one that is sometimes only truly understood by someone who shared it. Because we lived through all of it together, we were able to just be in each other's presence and somehow not have to explain anything. We still are, almost eight years later.

Jason, Karen, Cat, Steve, and Bill are still cherished friends whom I see whenever possible. Our families know and appreciate one another now as well. I would not trade our experiences together, nor our friendship today, for anything.

Of the many things you witnessed in Iraq, was there one that stood out as the most formative for you? What was it?

As long as I live, I will never forget being with Corporal Jason Dunham as he fought through a devastating brain injury, convincing us he was alive long enough to be sent home—to die according to his wishes, with his parents at his side.

Has the military's focus on mental health changed since your time in Iraq? In your opinion, how could the system be improved?

The DOD and VA systems have both made incredible strides in the awareness, understanding, detection, diagnosis, treatment, and maintenance of combat stress injuries in our country's service members. We have come a very long way since I returned in 2005. Progress is being made today with regard to new and complementary therapies that allow for increased quality of life, pain control, and symptom reduction. Providers are being trained in the evidence-based approaches to care and treatment. This is a marathon, and the treatment of our veterans will be a long and important road together. It will be worth the ongoing work of so many in order for us to get it right this time.

What was the process of writing Rule Number Two *like? How has your life been affected by its publication?*

Writing *Rule Number Two* was therapy, pure and simple. It saved me in multiple ways. I wrote it for my own healing, for my children and husband, and for Deb Dunham. The fact that its publication has led to so many getting in touch and telling me their stories has been a gift I could never have imagined.

My world has changed drastically since the publication of the book—it has led directly to my current work, which is now defined by forty to fifty invited presentations per year to many different audiences, from active-duty leaders to medical personnel to veterans' events to community organizations. I love public speaking and find each talk unique and rewarding in its ability to contribute to ongoing healing for all involved— our veterans, their families, their friends, their caregivers, and our country as a whole.

What do you most hope that readers will take away from reading about your experiences in Iraq? Has this changed at all in the five years since Rule Number Two *was first published?*

My hope has always been that the story would help raise awareness about our uniformed medical personnel serving in combat, and the unique risks and rewards facing them when they deploy. I hope that those who read the book will understand that, in many ways, we are all caregivers—and that our collective roles as such must extend to one another as we move through what will be a long road of healing and post-trauma growth—together.

Questions and topics for discussion

1. Before leaving for Iraq, Dr. Kraft writes, she was "always striving to separate the feelings of a clinician, who made decisions rationally and calmly, from those of a woman and mother, who sometimes did not" (8). When she arrives, she soon realizes that she won't be able to function if her children stay at the forefront of her consciousness, that there's a choice she has to make—combat psychologist or mother. Why is this? How does her decision play out during her time abroad?

2. Do you think one can ever feel ready for deployment? Why or why not?

3. Discuss the significance of Friday Night Fights. What was it about these three hours that made the men and women on the base feel transported home? What were some other ways that Dr. Kraft and her colleagues exerted control over their circumstances?

4. In "Convoy," Dr. Kraft writes, "For Marines, I thought, earning that [Combat Action] ribbon was a source of

genuine pride, almost a definition of the values for which they stand. Psychologists who care for Marines, especially in combat, needed to comprehend that fact" (74). What does she mean? How do you think Marines are different from the rest of us?

5. How did you interpret Dr. Kraft's "Eye in the Sky" dream? What do you think Jason means when he posits that it's the "fear that the protector could become the enemy" (49)? Do you agree with him?

6. At the end of the book, Dr. Kraft writes that her return "to seeing regular patients...could only be described as torture" (231). Why is this aspect of her daily life a challenge? How has her perspective changed during her months in Iraq?

7. Have you ever had to make a decision that required a life-changing sacrifice? What was it, and what were the consequences that outweighed the sacrifice?